COVER PHOTOGRAPHS

Top: BE 7217 Burrell 8 NHP 3 speed, No. 3057, built 1908. Worked in Linconshire; rebuilt by owner J. Sarney, High Wycombe.

E 9597 Burrell 5 NHP 3 speed, No. 3996, built 1924. Worked in Staffordshire; rebuilt by owner R. Sandercock, Stoke Climsland, Cornwall.

Bottom: CGB 777X Volvo F12 with fluid flywheel. 150 ton Gross Train weight, new 1982 with Tasker 120 ton trailer with 85 ton hull "Countess Fiona" from Stobcross crane, Glasgow to Balloch, Loch Lomond.

ACKNOWLEDGEMENTS

I would sincerely thank all those who helped both with information and photography, without whose help this book would never have been possible. My thanks are due especially to the F. Hal Higgins collection, University of California; Michael S. Moss, Archivist, University of Glasgow; John R. Hume, University of Strathclyde; R. F. Dell, the Strathclyde Regional Archivist and his staff; Murdoch Nicolson of the North British Locomotive Collection and staff of the Glasgow room in the Mitchell Library; S. A. S. Smith of Museum of Transport, Glasgow; J. L. Wood of the Royal Scottish Museum, Edinburgh; the family of the late T. C. Kerr, including his youngest daughter Mrs. Struthers and his grand-daughter Mrs. McDougall; the late George Mathers and his nephew Doctor Duncan K. M. Black; the late T. B. Paisley; the late John Trail; the school teacher in Struan school in the early 70's; the late D. Wilson Laing; Alex MacKinlay retired Pickfords Manager; William Lind, William Hamilton, Dan McKay, Alan Duke, Frank Strange, Alan Martin, R. G. Pratt, W. A. Briggs, P. G. Smart and the late Michael Salmon of the Road Locomotive Society; Iain Muir and the late Bill Oswald of the Scottish Traction Engine Society; Messrs Coats Patons Plc; R. W. M. Clouston, group archivist of Babcock International Plc; Messrs Pickfords Industrial Ltd; Messrs Weir Pumps Ltd; Messrs N. E. I. Peebles Ltd; Messrs Cadzow Plant Hire Ltd; Messrs Cochranes of Annan Ltd; Messrs Andrew Barclay Sons & Co Ltd; Messrs W. Ralston Ltd; Messrs John Young & Co (Kelvinhaugh) Ltd; Motherwell Bridge Fabricators Ltd; the Clyde Port Authority; Messrs McKelvie & Co Transport Ltd incorporating Strathclyde Transport.

T. McT.

PIONEERS OF HEAVY HAULAGE

This is first of all the story of the steam traction engine and the part it played in the history of heavy haulage in Scotland. This covers a span of a hundred years, from the early days when steam took over from horsepower and even manpower as the sole means of moving heavy loads, to the later days when the steam traction engine itself was superceded by petrol and diesel engines of ever increasing sophistication.

It is the story of the men and their machines and of the firms who flourished and their links with the heavy engineering companies, mainly of Glasgow and the Clydeside — the industrial heart of Scotland for so long.

THE WORKSHOP OF THE WORLD

In the early 19th century shipbuilding was booming all along the Clydeside. Boiler making and engine building, both for ship and also land installations, were rapidly expanding. All of these industries required the moving of heavy and sometimes massive loads. In these early days the engineering firms of the Clydeside used manpower to haul boilers and heavy machinery from foundry and erection shops to their installation points. Large numbers of men were involved. Between three and five hundred men were a normal number but on occasions as many as eight hundred men were needed. Ropes were attached to iron wheeled bogies with the men hauling the loads from place to place. This practise greatly added to the cost of the job as many of these men were engineers or boiler-makers who were taken from their skilled tasks simply to haul loads.

No reliable mechanical engine had as yet been invented. However, it was from a much older industry that the beginnings of our story are to be traced. Around 1830 the Highland Agricultural Society offered a prize of £500, a considerable sum at that time, for a "reliable ploughing engine". Inventors all over the country took up the challenge but without much success until in the mid 1860's a Mr. R. W. Thomson, Civil Engineer of Edinburgh produced a road steamer running on rubber tyres.

THE THOMSON STEAMER

Early one morning in the summer of 1865 R.W. Thomson demonstrated his road steamer to the Duke of Sutherland and Lord Dunaskin on the sandy sea shore at Portobello. They were so impressed by the performance of this massive three wheeled steam engine running over the soft sand in pouring rain — without sinking — that they immediately asked for ploughing trials to be carried out on farm land nearby. This proved a complete success and they each ordered an engine for their own use.

1. — Locomotive being man-hauled as most heavy loads were before the arrival of the Thomson road steamer.

2. — A very early photograph of a Thomson Road Steamer hauling a boiler at Leith Docks, 1868.

REVOLUTIONARY DESIGN

However, although designed primarily as a ploughing engine, it was soon found to be an ideal road haulage engine. Thomson's design was revolutionary in having solid rubber tyres which were not attached to, but ran loose inside the wheel rims. In effect the solid rubber tyres completed only one revolution while the engine covered a distance of one mile. The heat generated by friction caused something of a problem and the tyres occasionally vulcanised to the rims. Another problem had to be overcome by adding metal straps across the rubber tyres so protecting them from the flints used in road-making at that time. A simple two cylinder engine supplied the power to a two-speed gear box with top gear for empty running and low gear for road hauling.

No differential was fitted; instead, a dog clutch was fitted at each end of the drive shaft. When turning corners the dog clutch on the inside of the turning circle was disengaged. Water tanks to supply the boiler were fitted below and inside the frame between the front wheel and the firebox and also carried pannier-fashion on the outside of the frame.

The original model Thomson had a vertical pot boiler but this was later improved by fitting a vertical field boiler with tubes to enable a more even steam pressure to be maintained.

WORLD-WIDE SALES

Interest was shown in the new road steamer by the British Government. Following numerous exacting tests conducted by the Royal Woolwich Arsenal they were eventually completely satisfied that this was a suitable vehicle for their purposes — mainly for hauling heavy guns. Once this hurdle had been passed, orders flooded in from all over the world. Tennant of Leith was the Scottish builder, and three firms of traction engineers in England were licensed to build the road steamer — Messrs Robey of Lincoln, Messrs Ransomes, Sims & Head of Ipswich (who supplied Thomsons to the Indian Army) and Messrs Burrell of Thetford. A similar licence was granted for the U.S.A. to Williamson of New York City.

Employers in Glasgow had considered various types of road engines for load hauling but reliability and safety were serious problems. This was made evident only a few months before the arrival of the first Thomson in Glasgow.

An engine had been supplied by John Yule & Company to Messrs Elder of Govan to haul machinery to one of the harbour cranes. When returning for a second load it stopped to take on water in Paisley Road. The boiler exploded. Ten people were killed and fifty more were seriously injured.

Thomsons had been used to haul boilers and

other machinery in and around Edinburgh for about 3 years before they went into use in Glasgow. The first Thomson to arrive in Glasgow was a 12 Nominal Horse Power engine built by Tennant of Leith for Captain Lou-sada R.N. (retired). This engine was to remain part of the Clydeside scene for sixty years. Arriving in 1872, it was joined by another in 1873.

Elder of Govan (later Fairfields) purchased an 8 NHP Thomson and found it useful for moving small loads, but not for the big lifts. Later they sold it to Lou-sada who by this time had formed a company called The Road Steam Engine Company of 146 Lancefield Street, Glasgow. Managed by Mr. J. C. Brown the business prospered, requiring more and more engines to cope with their increasing business.

In 1875 Mr. D. F. Laurie Fogo bought into the Company, and became managing director of the new Limited Company. Shortly afterwards, three new Thomsons were purchased — 2 of 12 NHP and one of 8 NHP, making a total of six steamers. Meanwhile another two 12 NHP Thomsons built at Tennants in 1868/9 were bought from Mr. White of Kettocks Mill, three miles from Aberdeen. They had proved to be too heavy for Mr. White's work. So six of 12 NHP and two of 8 NHP became the fleet which ran until 1914 before another new engine was purchased.

EVEN THOMSONS HAD THEIR PROBLEMS

Captain Lou-sada in correspondence with Lieutenant R.E. Crompton of the Indian Army who had a number of Thomsons built at Ransomes, Sims and Head of Ipswich noted that the Pot boilers fitted originally had to be replaced by Field boilers as the Pots were not popular even with the Insurance Company. He also stated that the driving wheel tyres lasted two years and cost between £195 and £200 from the North British Rubber Company of Edinburgh. The front wheel tyres carrying no weight had at that time never been replaced. There were mechanical problems but manager Mr. W. Marshall explained another fundamental problem — that of restriction of movement — in another letter to Lieutenant Crompton:

Within the dock area and the adjacent streets the steamers could move freely but there was considerable restriction on their movements through the city centre in daylight hours. Futhermore cross-river traffic over the bridges on the Clyde was severely limited.

The Bridge Trustees had placed restrictions on the weights and vehicles that might cross the bridges. For example, regulations did not admit of any traction engines, even without loads, crossing by Broomielaw Bridge. While on the Victoria and Albert bridges the Trustees limited the weight of the whole train; engines, bogies and load to a maximum of 60 tons.

As a 12 NHP Thomson weighed 11 tons, the bogie approximately 8 tons, this left only 41 tons for the load. Now a 40 ton load on a normal haul would require three engines. So when crossing the bridge, two tracing engines would be uncoupled, leaving one engine to struggle over the bridge before coupling on the other two again at the other side.

TRAFFIC INCREASES

While these regulations may of themselves have been prudent the affects were detrimental to the interests of shipbuilders, marine engineers and ship owners alike at a time when the volume and frequency of loads being carried was rising rapidly. In the three years 1873/75 the loads taken to the sixty-ton crane at Finnieston and the seventy-ton south bank crane at Plantation Quay were never above 50 tons and only fifty loads were above 40 tons. But by 1881/1883 the number of loads over 40 tons was upwards of two hundred and fifty, while some were over 60 tons.

Messrs John Elder during the three years ending June 1883, put into vessels no fewer than one hundred and twenty loads, each weighing over 40 tons, of which forty-five were over 50 tons and twenty over 60 tons in weight.

In 1883 Mr. Marshall attended a bridge building enquiry confirming the weights of loads carried and stated that between two and three thousand loads weighing about 40,000 tons were moved per annum, involving 6,000 engine journeys in the course of a year. Single journeys between the north and south of the city in the same period were in excess of 2,500.

FITTING OUT PROBLEMS

Traffic across the bridges would have been greatly increased had the bridges been opened without limits since the necessity of harbour works often caused the ships to be berthed at the opposite side of the river from the machinery works from which they were loading.

The situation often resulted in the south side cranes being slack from want of work while those on the north side had difficulty keeping up with the demand. Sometimes it was the other way round, but the result was the same: delays in the turn-round time taken to fit out the ships with boilers and engines.

For instance in 1883, the Dominion Line Steamer "Vancouver," a vessel of 6,000 tons could not get a turn, as quickly as required, at one of the north-side cranes to receive machinery from the works of J & J Thomson across the river at Finnieston Street. So, as a consequence she had to be berthed at the Plantation crane on the southside of the river thus involving greater expense and delay in moving the machinery from the works by road and bridge a distance of over 2 miles as against 300 yards. When less than half the machinery had been transported it was found that the load weights of the remainder were in excess of what the bridge trustees would allow to cross and the completion of the vessel was further delayed until a berth could be obtained at one of the northside cranes. The Lord Provost McOnie, himself an engineer, enquired of Mr. Marshall what he considered a bridge should be able to carry. At least 150 tons was the

3. — Two teams of 8NHP and 12NHP Thomsons hauling boilers at Glasgow. Approx. 1890.

recommendation. This was later taken into consideration when the bridges were rebuilt.

CRANAGE INCREASES

In 1895 a new fixed jib steam crane came into operation at Finnieston able to lift 130 tons. Across the river, Princes Dock a new wet dock, was constructed and on the south wall another 130 tons crane known as the Whitefield Road Crane came into operation two years later. The 70 ton crane at Plantation was also rebuilt with wire rope instead of chain lifting equipment.

Now the upper reaches of the Clyde had the old 60 ton and the new 130 ton cranes at Finnieston, along with the two southside cranes bringing them to a peak at which they remained for thirty-five years until 1932 when the hammer-head came into operation.

MORE FIRMS IN COMPETITION

Captain Lou-sada left the Road Steam Engine Company to become Manager of Glasgow Tramway Company in the early 1890's. The Road Steam Engine Company in common with other general hauliers suffered from newcomers coming into business cutting rates to gain traffic. In the long run this destroyed the newcomers as well as the established firms.

4. — Five 12NHP Thomsons and an 8NHP Aveling hauling a 131 ton diesel engine from D. Rowans to the 130 ton crane at Finnieston, Glasgow, 1919.

In 1890 a firm of steam pipe coverers Reid and McFarlane of 58 Hydepark Street bought two second-hand traction engines and advertised them for hire. They traded for ten years. How much work they did is not known, but they folded up in 1900.

These same two traction engines then appeared under the name of McFarlane & Son, Engineers of 153 Elliot Street. They later moved premises to Shieldhall about five miles away on the other side on the river. The firm closed down in 1928, selling the only vehicle left, a 5 ton Foden wagon No. 7932 registration number M9605.

In 1899 P & W MacLellan & Co., Structural Engineers of 129 Trongate provided traction engines for hire. They only lasted until 1906, in that field. The Road Steam Engine Company struggled on but it was not until March 1913 that a new 8 NHP road locomotive (No. 7941) built by Aveling and Porter was added to the fleet and the two small Thomsons were scrapped. Bogies remained the same as the man-hauled originals. The company carried on until 1932 when eventually the slump caught up with them.

WILLIAM KERR & COMPANY

Meanwhile a new company had entered the field, one which was to become a dominant force. This business William Kerr & Co., Machinery Merchants and Brokers, Greenbank Street, Mavisbank was owned and run by Thomas Currie Kerr who used his father's name to register the business. T. C. Kerr born in 1868 was 32 years of age when he put his first engine on the road.

T.C. Kerr was the first of three outstanding figures to appear on the heavy haulage scene. The second was Norman E. Box of Manchester who appeared in 1907 and worked in conjunction with Kerr and the third who did not appear until the late 1920's was "Bubbly" Bob Young of John Young & Co. In April 1899 T. C. Kerr purchased an 8 NHP Burrell No. 2088 named *Charlie* a four wheeled heavy bogie with a single iron wheel at each corner of a rectangular oak frame reinforced by iron corner plates. The frame was approximately twelve feet long by six feet wide. The wheels ran on solid axles which required frequent oiling. No method of braking was required — when the engine stopped pulling, the trailer came to a standstill. In fact this characteristic was the same on all bogies from the days when they were man-hauled.

He also purchased a coal trailer which had to carry timbers and tackle for erection work as well as coal.

5. — Two Thomsons 12NHP with marine boiler 1920's.

6. — 1906, 10NHP Burrell No. 1997 "Lord Roberts" of William Kerr & Co. with Lancashire boiler.

Kerr started his young brother James as outside erecting foreman and within a year another two men joined them. They contracted to deliver and erect into working position, Lancashire, Cornish and vertical boilers constructed by Penman & Co. of Dalmarnock, Glasgow. At this time many collieries and a variety of manufacturing industries were opening up across Scotland. Not all the boilers travelled by road, some smaller ones were moved by rail to their nearest destination, then Kerr transferred them from the railway to the works.

Lancashire boilers were by far the most popular. They came in various sizes, the largest being thirty feet long by ten feet in diameter with twin flues running the full length of the boiler. Cornish boilers were of lesser diameter with only a single flue running the full length. Penman & Co. built only a few vertical boilers as they were too busy with the big lanky boilers. Later Wilson of Lilybank, moved from Eglinton Toll to London Road, and opened up in opposition to Penman & Co. giving more work than ever to Kerr's.

LORD ROBERTS ARRIVES

In March 1903 Kerr purchased the *Lord Roberts* a second hand 2 speed Burrell showmans road locomotive No. 1997 which had been built in July, 1897 for a North Wales showman. Having a 7" x 11.1/2" diameter cylinders she rated 10 NHp.

With the additional engine he also acquired a new trailer for long distance work. This was a flat trailer of two chassis beams with six cross beams all of steel, mounted on double axles. the rear wheels were of a larger diameter than the front and again the wheels were of iron and unshod. This trailer replaced the original solid bogie outside the City of Glasgow where the bogie made short work of the unmade road surfaces.

Charlie was used to trace *Lord Roberts* with the load to its destination where it was unloaded using the two engines, one on either side, with the winch wire over the top of the boiler and shackled to the trailer. One pulled and the other held back dropping the boiler on to two loose axles with two small iron wheels each. This was used to put the boiler on to its foundation using the winch on *Charlie*, the bigger engine returning with the big trailer to Glasgow for further use.

A NEW APPROACH

T. C. Kerr was already an expert on the valuation and handling of boilers and machinery. He recognised the advantages of having outside erection squads working with haulage engines when no other contractor supplied this service. He changed the order of boiler installation, instead of the boilermaker's own men being responsible, now they only coupled up the pipes and were present at the first steaming.

This side of the business moved forward in leaps and bounds. In 1906 James Kerr and his squad were in Portugal erecting the steelwork for the J. & P. Coats Ltd., thread mill at Quinta de Cravel, three miles south of Oporto. This job was complete in 1907 in time to ship out to Brazil to erect a mill at Sao Paulo ready for opening in 1908. Then it was off to Ireland to undertake a number of boiler installations before setting sail for Portugal again, this time to fit out a power station.

Meantime other squads were erecting and installing boilers at home in Scotland, working from Kerr's yard at Mavisbank and another yard was rented in Scotland Street about half a mile distant to hold additional equipment.

Robert Kerr, another brother of T. C.'s started work with the company. He had been 1st officer on a tramp streamer and had lost an eye while chipping rust.

7. — 1911 in St. Petersburg, T.C. Kerr on right of boiler, supervising Russian workers.

His job was to check the sizes of the load and make sure the route planned was suitable so as not to waste time. A pony and trap was his main conveyance.

The next engine to arrive was a 7 NHP Foden No. 771 named *Thistle* from Alan Meikle of Mount Vernon in 1906. It lasted only a year as it was found to be too light for the work. A new Fowler B7 No. 11271 arrived in October 1907 having 6.3/4" x 11.1/2" diameter cylinders, another 10 NHP engine. She took over from *Lord Roberts* for out of town work. Unfortunately although they worked together for a few years they were not suited for one another and it was not until No. 2105 a 10 NHP Burrell with 7" x 11.1/2" diameter cylinders arrived in January 1912 that it was possible to get two Burrells working together again.

ST. PETERSBURG CONTRACT

In July 1911 J & P Coats Ltd., chartered a ship to sail to Russia to carry everything needed to build a five-storey thread mill.This included all the steelwork, boilers, engine, looms. Mr J. Aspin, Messrs Coats' agent, arranged to ship Kerr's erection equipment and his men, James Kerr, the two Holmes brothers James and Peter, along with a few skilled erectors and bricklayers to St. Petersburg in Russia. J. Aspin and T. C. Kerr, their wives and Kerr's youngest daughter travelled overland, arriving before the chartered ship.

T. C. arranged for the foundations to be started and additional labour taken on and delegated to different squads. Working a three shift system, six days a week, the mill was completed in the astonishing time of 13 weeks, to beat the Russian winter. One of the problems facing the foreman early on was that the local workers liked a half-pint of Vodka with their lunch, and thought they could sleep after it. The Holmes brothers who could drink a distillery dry everyday and still do the work, soon sorted them out. The Czar of all the Russians was so delighted with T. C. Kerr's accomplishment that he presented him with a silver sugar and cream set, inlaid with enamel and lined with gold.

SELFRIDGES

Other jobs were taken on in the London area including the erection of a main post office and Selfridges in Oxford Street. Erecting steelwork was done using a pole like a derrick with a powered winch, probably then a traction engine winch.

T. C. Kerr had a season ticket on the railway for London, spending two or three days a week in the area. He also had a season for Manchester where he was for two days per week, as he was a director of the Enfield Cable Co. As some of his men were away from home for a long period he visted their families in case they needed anything. This was a feature of the company right up to nationalisation, the Boss visited wives and mothers to ensure their welfare and to put the men's mind at rest.

With the coming of the 10 NHP Burrell, the Fowler joined the *Lord Roberts* doing short hauls with single engine loads. Many boilers were moved and erected in the Glasgow district using *Lord Roberts* solo with a bogie similar to the original, except that it had a

8. — Early 1912 W. Kerr's fleet of a 10NHP Fowler, Burrell "Lord Roberts",
Burrell 8NHP "Charlie" and Burrell 10 NHP No. 2105.

turning lock and using 12 foot drawbars could carry the thirty feet long boilers. A few of these boilers were launched into the River Clyde then towed by a small tugboat to the various islands off the West Coast of Scotland. Anchored off the shore Kerr's squad hauled it ashore, placing it in the two loose axles to haul it by hand-winch to the gas works, distillery or wherever. The Lancashire boiler was very popular as it could burn most fuels, including sawdust although it was very hard to get any useful steam pressure at all with this type of fuel.

THE MIGHTY CLYDE

An order was placed with Charles Burrell of Thetford to supply a 10 NHP contractors type road locomotive with Kerr supplying a cast steel perch bracket and front axle. Special fitments included 7/8" diameter high tensile wire rope for winching, with a cast steel winch drum. This was the largest engine to be

9. — 1915. Bottom half of Turbine hauled by an 8NHP Burrell "Charlie" of W. Kerr
and an 8NHP Aveling of the Road Steam Engine Co.

built by Burrell for road use in this country (although 16 NHP engines had been built for use in Brazil.) With cylinder sizes of 7.1/4" x 11.3/4" she was nearer 12 NHP than 10. Number 3419 was delivered in October 1912 and named *Clyde*. When registration was brought in, in 1920, she received GA7818. With the arrival of *Clyde*, Kerr was now in a position to quote for other haulage work normally done by the Road Steam Engine Co. Prior to this Kerr was fully employed with the haulage and erection of boilers and other machines — work that the Road Steam Engine Co. did not do. William Kerr & Co. also expanded into other work including marine boilers and it was not an unusual sight in Glasgow to see a train of traction engines hauling a big boiler through the streets.

ALAN MEIKLE

Another contractor supplying engines was Alan Meikle of Tollcross, Glasgow, who had one traction engine on constant hire to William Beardmore & Co., Parkhead Forge, for the moving of odd-shaped castings, rudders, stern frames etc., and one engine on general work which included boiler haulage, usually about 20 tons maximum load. Kerr became the leading boiler haulier south of the river with the Road Steam Engine Co. operating the north side.

Messrs Barclay Curle, shipbuilders and engineers had two boilershops as well as an engineering shop and a shipyard. One of the boilershops was at the foot of Whitefield Road right across the road from the 130 ton crane. This boilershop concentrated on export work with weights of up to 120 tons. The bogies used were still the same as the man-hauled type used before 1872, with a wheel at each corner. Although with the advent of the 120 tonner the bogie wheels were increased to eight, they were still without a steering lock. Boilers were loaded by daylight and after the last tram the Corporation Tramway Department's overhead wiremen lifted the wires, pegging them up in slots provided on the standards. When the boilers were across the road the wiremen returned the wires to the normal height in time for the first tram. The 100 to 120 tonners required four traction engines to haul them, but if Thomsons were used it would require five or six as they were much lighter.

One may wonder why the roads could carry such massive loads, as much as 35 tons to a wheel when it is only about 2.1/2 tons today. The reason was that the streets of Glasgow and district were specially constructed to carry this traffic. Whinstone bottoming was placed down first and then two inch down whin was rolled in then concreted with sand placed on top as a foundation for the granite setts which were held in position by tar in the seams.

THE HOUSE OF LORDS

In 1919 the Glasgow Corporation Highways Department issued a writ against Messrs Barclay Curle for loads from their Kelvinhaugh Street boiler shop damaging the road at the top of Finnieston Street when enroute to the 130 ton Finnieston crane. This traffic was carried by Wm. Kerr although it was on the north side. The case went to the House of Lords in

10. — 4 ton Foden No. 6912, Registration No. M9127 new 10/2/1917 W. Kerr & Company.

11. — W. Kerr's four Burrells of 1919 with a 120 ton boiler.
This is a load similar to Barclay Curle v The Glasgow Corporation Roads Department case heard in the House of Lords in 1919.

1920. During the hearing of the case it was asked what tonnage was delivered to the Finnieston crane in a year. No one could give even an estimate, but the Road Steam Engine Co. who were not directly involved volunteered the information that they had delivered a diesel engine from D. Rowan of Elliot Street, weighing 131 tons in one movement. The House of Lords verdict was for Barclay Curle ruling that the Corporation had to construct roadways fit to carry the local trade.

A DANGEROUS JOB

In those days most enginemen and their helpers had toes missing and bits out of their legs caused by the tops of the granite setts flying off while a bogie was being dragged around a corner. The reason that the bogies were not changed sooner was to keep the overall height down below the tram wires. Had a steering lock been incorporated it would have raised the height to beyond the tram wires. These bogies were also easily coupled together for long loads. Although shipyards on

12. — "Clyde" with 30 tons bottom half turbine gear case. Always delivered upside down, when machined on the faces and turned up would not require turning again. Early 1920's.

13. — W. Kerr's Fowler with 19 ton cylinder casting at Fullerton, Hodgart & Barclay's foundry in Paisley.
Early 1920's.

14. — Alan Meikle of Tollcross's Garrett super heated traction engine No. 28375 built 1910
with a sixteen ton boiler for trawler.

the East coast continued to build hulls they did not build engines or boilers. These were built on the Clydeside and shipped to the customer on steam lighters known on the west coast as puffers. Puffers could carry 100 tons and were small enough to sail through the Forth and Clyde Canal and just big enough for the North Sea, weather permitting, sailing to yards in Leith, Burntisland, Dundee, Aberdeen, and on occasion Tyneside.

NIGHT WORK

The Alma Boiler Works was located in Crownpoint Road in the east end of Glasgow. They built mostly marine boilers, but also on occasion, Economy and Lancashire boilers. The big marine boilers could not travel through the city by day without a holdup of normal traffic. Instead they ran after the last tram at night and normally they came in two's; as overhead wiremen were in attendance it was nearly as easy with two as with one.

THE HAMMERHEADS

Up to 1910 most ships were engined at one of the harbour cranes. Then one or two of the yards started building their own hammerheads. Messrs Fairfield built a 200 tonner followed by Barclay Curle and then John Browns. In 1915 Harland and Wolff bought over two small shipyards in Govan merging them into one big yard and Messrs W Beardmore had a shipyard and engineering shop at Dalmuir where they also had a fitting-out crane.

SKIRTING THE CANALS

Central Scotland was cut in two by the Forth and Clyde Canal which, although skirting Glasgow, had a port within 300 yards of George Square in the centre of the city. Port Dundas had been constructed to be the Glasgow end of the Monkland Canal which ran from Caldercruix in the heart of Lanarkshire, passing through the iron belt in Calderbank and Coatbridge. There the barges were loaded for the city. A branch from the Forth and Clyde joined into Port Dundas. These canals did not make out-of-the-city delivery easy as the majority of roads had only 3 ton bridges. The canal owners objected to heavier bridges being built as they could see the steam vehicles undercutting their traffic just as the railways had done in the last century. In time however heavy canal bridges were constructed at Dalmuir to allow heavy lifts to travel to Dumbarton and at Castle Street in Glasgow over the Monkland Canal. With an aquaduct over the far end of Maryhill Road any Lancashire boilers going to Stirlingshire, Fife, Perthshire and the North East had to make a wide detour via Milngavie, Strathblane, Lennoxtown to Kilsyth keeping north of the canal.

It was 1926 before the Castlecary Canal bridge on the main Glasgow to Stirling road was rebuilt to carry 200 tons also the Riddrie bridge over the Monkland Canal was reconstructed to carry 200 tons. Other bridges on main roads were also upgraded.

15. — Not an advertisement for beer.
"Clyde" and McLaren GA7821 with Penman Lancashire boiler on the road 1920's.

16. — Cumming of Paisley with two Foden wagons and three Sentinels
with gas works equipment from A.F. Craig of Paisley.

17. — The "Anzac" steam lighter known as a Puffer. These little boats were specially suitable for Scottish inshore waters
and were used to carry engines and boilers through the Forth/Clyde canal to the East Coast.

18. — Hauling locomotives to the railway.
Andrew Barclay of Kilmarnock, 1902 using a
Burrell S.C.C. Traction Engine.

With the Great War starting in 1914 general heavy haulage increased dramatically. Although Kerr's had been started for the haulage of boilers they were soon invloved in a wide variety of other heavy work. To help out with the additional work vehicles were acquired — seven Foden 5 ton steam wagons No. 2396, Reg. No. M2687 bought second hand in 1914; No. 2962, Reg. No. M2962, No. 5876, Reg. No. M8456, No. 6070, Reg. No. M8458 and No. 6140, Reg. No. M8462 all second hand in 1916; No. 6554 Reg. No. M8923 second hand in 1916 No. 6912, Reg. No. M9127 new in February 1917; also an Aveling and Porter 8 NHP No. 5012 in November 1915 were purchased.

Kerrs had an engine working in Port Glasgow and Greenock with several bogies hauling between engine and boiler shops to the fitting-out crane in Victoria harbour in Greenock. It spent most of the year there calling to Glasgow for assistance with heavy lifts. James Kerr and the outside erecting squads spent a lot of time fitting out ordnance factories with machinery, boilers and steel chimneys. A number of the steam wagons were employed on this work. Stern and rudder frames from Wm. Beardmore normally moved by Alan Meikle with his little Garrett were given to Kerrs for transport to Greenock, Irvine, Troon, Ayr, Dumbarton and Leith. The Steel Company of Scotland at Hallside near Cambuslang also cast sternframes, rudders and odd castings; Kerrs also acquired this traffic. The West of Scotland was also the centre of the sugar cane crushing machinery building industry. Four firms were engaged in this work and they all passed their heavy work to Kerr.

19. — Boilers loading at Alma boiler works in the East End of Glasgow by day-light
to be moved by night after the last tram. Late 1920's.

20. — Nightshift in Argyle Street in the rain with overhead wiremen in attendance.
"Clyde" and a McLaren.

21. — Another 120 ton boiler on eight wheeled bogie being hauled by four Burrells
of W. Kerr at the Whitefield Road Crane, 1925.

22. — Fullerton, Hodgart & Barclay Ltd. Paisley built mine winding machinery. "Clyde" and "Lord Roberts" with crankshaft bound for South Africa 1930.

23. — Burrell "Clyde" and a McLaren coupling up to trailer "Loch Ness Monster" with 80 ton India-bound locomotive leaving Queen's Park works (Old Dubs Works) at U turn from gate, 1930.

24. — Double trailer movement for China.

THE ROAD TO LONDON

Transporting loads longer distances was not a simple matter. For example, the road to Edinburgh had a restricted bridge over the Monkland Canal in Coatbridge. So the route taken meant a wide detour through Tollcross to Mount Vernon then left through Bellshill, Holytown to Newhouse, left to Airdrie, Caldercruix, Bathgate, Uphall and Broxburn etc. into Edinburgh. Loads going to England used the same route, then down the A1 to Newcastle where they had to drop down on to the quayside, crossing the swingbridge then climb up into Gateshead, travelling further south on the A1 to London or wherever. Any loads bound for the Mersey were taken by ship instead of ballast for the run down the Irish Sea.

The road from Annan to Glasgow was so bad that Messrs Cochrane of Annan who made boilers of all descriptions and also built Ruth's Accumulators sent what they could by rail. But some of the boilers and Ruth's equipment weighed as much as 70 tons and anything that could not travel by rail was launched into the Solway and towed by tug to its destination. Cochranes were doing this as late as 1931. Kerr's used the crane in Victoria Harbour Greenock to load a 65 ton accumulator which had been towed up from Annan for Westburn Sugar Refinery.

PEAK TIME FOR TRACTION ENGINES

At the end of the First World War in 1918/19 one 8 NHP McLaren No. 595 built May 1897, and three 10 NHP McLarens No. 1600 built November 1917, No. 1627 built July 1918 and No. 1594 of October 1917 G6804, were purchased from the War Department. The round military tenders were replaced with the normal commercial tender. Early in the 1920's a 6 NHP Foster No. 14189 Reg No. AG4137, built May 1920 fitted with crane, was bought second hand. This was the peak the firm was to reach with the post war boom collapsing, a collapse which brought the closure of shipyards, boiler, engine shops and engineering works, some never to re-open.

ELSEWHERE IN SCOTLAND

Strange to relate outside of Glasgow and the Clydeside heavy haulage was practically unknown although Thomsons were used to haul small boilers and later on a steam wagon would have moved light loads.

However in Aberdeen, the Shore Porters Society continued the practice of hiring out gangs of men with the old four wheel bogies to move loads in and around the harbour area. This practise was continued right up until 1930 though latterly an engine would be hired from local quarry masters for the more difficult moves.

25. — Another China bound locomotive leaving Queen's Park on double trailers with two Burrells and a McLaren. 1930.

26. — Fowler of W. Kerr hauling a sugar cane crushing roller, 1930.

27. — Indian locomotive en route to docks 1930 hauled by
"Clyde" and "Lord Roberts".

28. — Indian locomotive being lifted off trailers. In the background are centre portions of Garrett articulated locomotives for Kenya-Uganda railway built under licence by the North British Locomotive Co. Ltd., 1931.

29. — Steam accumulator built at Annan and launched into the Solway Firth to be towed to Greenock. June 1931.

29a. — Back on dry land the accumulator is en-route from
Victoria Harbour to Westburn Sugar Refinery, Greenock.

30. — Now the 69 ton accumulator is manoeuvred round a corner — with difficulty —
as the steel wheeled bogies were without turning locks.

In 1926 Tom C Kerr designed a trailer which was built to order from P & W McLellan of Glasgow. This trailer was to run until 1951. It was built to carry 150 tons, being constructed of steel with a cranked frame, a 36 foot well and ran on 16 iron wheels. Shortly afterwards a second trailer was purchased with a 20 foot well. These two trailers were used bolted back-to-back for the long railway locomotives then coming from the works.

From 1926 on to 1939 the North British Loco produced so many locos for shipment that Kerr's big trailer nicknamed the *Loch Ness Monster*, worked on many occasions night and day as the locos were delivered to the two 130 ton steam cranes and on occasion to the 70 ton crane at Clyde Villa on the south bank of the Clyde.

Do not let the reader be confused with the running weight of a loco as this included the weight of the tender, fuel and water. The loco when transported rarely was over 100 tons — more usually around 90 tons plus 25 tons on the tender. Articulated locomotives were split into two or three pieces, since most were delivered by ship to a port without heavy cranage where they required to be off-loaded using the ship's heavy derrick, known as a Jumbo.

In 1932 a new electric hammerhead 175 ton crane came into service at Stobcross Quay, two hundred yards west of the 130 ton Finnieston steam crane which had been built in 1895. Both cranes continued to be used for shipping locos or fitting out ships.

The trailer *Loch Ness Monster* had new wheels fitted in 1930. These were rubber tyres and ran on brass bushes. No brakes had been fitted originally and none were added right up until she was scrapped in 1951. The minute the engines stopped pulling, the trailer stopped too; even going down a slight gradient it just stopped. the tare was 36 tons and when coupled back to back with the other trailer of 25 tons, equalled 61 tons before the load went on. When the rubber tyres were fitted only two axles at the rear could be used as the trailer refused to turn at corners. Also when using double trailers on a dry day the fire tender had to be in attendance to hose the cobbles to allow the wheels to slide around the corners.

NIGHTS TO REMEMBER

At 11.55 p.m. at Queens Park Locomotive Works in Polmadie one night in 1931, 'Lord Roberts' pulled up outside the big gate on the corner opposite Brechins Bar with two clear hurricane lamps hanging from the front axle and two red hurricane lamps dancing behind the crank-framed trailer. As the gate opened, in the distance could be seen two other traction engines, 'Clyde' and a 10 NHP McLaren (they kept changing the number plates around as only two were road fund taxed) and behind them a huge railway locomotive mounted on two trailers. 'Lord Roberts' pulled into the yard and reversed his trailer into an adjacent door in the big bay to load the tender.

Polmadie slept on — but not for long! Bowler hatted managers chatted to the driver. Yellow coated foremen checked the boxmakers work in scotching the loco's wheels. Flagmen lit hurricane lamps to adorn the monster loco. Outside in the street as the last tram left the terminus, the fire tender proceeded to couple up the hoses. Two tower wagons arrived to lift the tram wires at the junctions where they sometimes sagged, then a police car and various Corporation Officials from the tramways, the Water Department and the Roads Department. The tower wagon crew went inside to measure the height of the loco. The double trailers were standing nose in; they had to come out backwards as there was a U-turn at the big gate and the two trailers could not be turned there. 'Clyde' and the McLaren were coupled on the rear and a second McLaren coupled on the front to steer it out.

When the tender was loaded and scotched 'Clyde's' driver, Watty Muir pulled the whistle and three throttles opened. Off they went to the gate where the local police constable assisted the mobile police to control the non existent traffic. Polmadie was awakening! Get up and get the dishes off the shelves before they are knocked off. Hoses in action, out she came cutting the corner. She is not going to make it! Stop! Ease her back! One bar off and turn the lock a bit, shunt the engines over a few feet, couple up pull! and round she came. Up the road a hundred yards to get the trailers straight, then uncouple and change the engines around, with 'Clyde' on the load at the front and one McLaren tracing and the other back-shoving.

They moved away with the fire tender in front, then the tower wagons, then the police, the monster followed by 'Lord Roberts' with the tender, then the Officials car in the rear to spy any damage done to water mains, tram track or roadway. Polmadie went back to sleep as the procession moved down to Cathcart Road where the overhead men watched their wires, the firemen hosed the crossing for the right turn. Down to the Gushet, hold well to the left and the wiremen will not need to lift the wires. But at Cumberland Street and Gorbals Street they had to lift them, then hoses out as a hard left turn is negotiated. Round she goes and the fire tender makes for home as it is now a straight run to the Whitefield Road crane in Govan which with wire lifting takes the remainder of the night. As they drew into the dock the first tram of the morning passed by. Then uncoupling, when the trailers were in the radius of the crane, which was marked with granite sets in a circle as the crane had a fixed jib. The engines were damped down for the dayshift to unload, then return the trailers to Polmadie for a repeat performance.

31. — Part of articulated locomotive moving from Hydepark Works to docks . . .

Both Kerrs and the Road Steam Engine Company used two single coupling bars instead of Vee bars. This gave the engines more manoeuvre ability. Uncoupling one bar and placing a hook into the eye of the other bar and with three large chain links attached to the hook, coupling a link to the rear coupling, the trailer would swing wide on a corner to save hauling it around with chains as was the normal procedure with a Vee bar.

Also when pulling a load two coupling pins were used instead of one. When an engine was back shoving on the front, the smoke box coupling would only take one pin. A butterfly transfer coupling was designed (so-called as it resembled one in shape) with a hole at the head to couple on to the smoke box and on each wing a hole to couple onto each bar. Originally the two bars were trued up to the single pin with one bar on top of the coupling and a large bolt and a nut used to secure them. Unfortunately on occasion, the nut unscrewed itself and one bar disappeared through the smoke box door, hence the need for the butterfly.

Springburn, strange to relate, was entirely different to Polmadie. Polmadie had no interest in locomotives except that they disturbed their sleep. Very few local men worked there; most came from Springburn or travelled from Lanarkshire. Springburn was a railway town inside the City of Glasgow and was only four miles from Polmadie.There, Hydepark workers met Atlas, Cowlairs and St. Rollox workers in pubs, churches and social clubs and passed the news around when a loco was moving at night. Out they came in their hundreds to pass judgement on the latest product of Springburn. Had they not built locos for nearly every country in the World! It was their product whether they worked for the Caledonian Railway, the North British Railway or the North British Locomotive it was Springburn built!

The Hydepark works were originally built in 1862 with direct access to the main railway line. The fitting and test bay was built facing the main line but was at a right angle to Vulcan Street, the road out of the works. Through the years this bay was enlarged with heavier cranes erected but it still meant that locos going by road had to make a tight right-angle turn. As exports increased in size it became an increasing problem getting double trailers around, this corner, into the tunnel, under the head office, and out into the street. The double trailers were nosed in to the despatch but this time without an engine inside the bay. The rear of the two trailers were bolted together. The two pairs of rear wheels were only about 10 feet apart and these were run on to steel plates, greased to pivot the centre of the trailers when the lock at each end was put hard round. With an engine at each end it was accomplished without too much bother but it took some time.

The Springburn folk watched and nodded approvingly as the convoy stopped outside the Railway

Mission Hall in Vulcan Street to await the arrival of the fire tender, the overhead wire men and the police. The wire men checked the height for the tram wires under Inchbelly bridge. Off they went after the firemen had hosed the corner into Springburn Road and down past St. Rollox works with the last of the spectators left behind. Into Parliamentary Road, lift the wires, down through Sauchiehall Street with hardly a passerby about, through Charing Cross, hoses out, turn left down North Street, hoses out right into St. Vincent Street, left into Finnieston Street and the 130 ton steam crane. This took all night — a distance of about five miles.

THE DEPRESSION

By now the depression was beginning to bite. In 1928 six Foden steam wagons were scrapped by Kerr's and in the same year McFarlane & Company went into liquidation. Kerr purchased from them a five ton Foden wagon No. 7932, Reg. No. M9605 built in 1918. The only firm left in competition to Kerrs was the Road Steam Engine Company.

A. F. CRAIG OF PAISLEY

Some customers had occasionally light bulky loads that went with a heavy lift. Kerr had used his Fodens on this type of work. One such firm was A. F. Craig of Paisley who built gasworks equipment, mixers and tanks as well as marine boilers, engines and various machines. It was usual to subcontract this work to contractors who operated steam wagons or the customer dealt direct with those firms who would supply vehicles for up to fifteen tons. William Cumming of Paisley operated eight steam wagons: Foden No. F6772 Reg. No. M9023 1916, Foden No. F7558 Reg. No. M9412 1917, Atkinson Reg No. CK3060 1918, Atkinson Reg. No. CK3060 1918, Sentinel No. 5749 Reg. No. GB6951 1924, Sentinel No. 8014 Reg. No. AG4697 1929, Sentinel No. A2525 Reg. No. AW5405 1919, Sentinel No. 8523 Reg. No. GG3843 1931. Using either a monkey or a four wheeled trailer was a common sight to see those vehicles running into the docks with odd shaped loads.

BLEAK INDUSTRIAL SCENE

P & W McLellan had built four new trailers for Kerr's since 1926, two flats, an extendable crank-framed 40 tonner and a thirty foot well, crank-framed trailer, six feet shorter than the *Loch Ness Monster*. But in 1929 another Foden was removed from Kerrs licence which left only the new purchase, No. 7932, in service. The Aveling and Porter and the Foster crane engine were also sold. This left the four Burrells, four McLarens (not all licensed), one Fowler, the Foden wagon and the trailers. The outside squads were now employed mainly in England and South America.

The industrial scene on the Clyde was now bleak with Lithgow of Port Glasgow importing stern frames from Germany, cheaper than they could be cast in Glasgow. Only an occasional big job moved in

32. — . . . and arriving at Clyde Villa 70 ton crane. Hauled by "Clyde", 1931.

33. — Another 1932 Chinese railway order on double trailers
which weighed 64 tons before loading the locomotive.

33a. — Turning the trailers in Hydepark Works
to line them up for the outward tunnel under the offices.

Greenock, the locomotives from the North British Locomotive Co. giving a bit of work. Barclay Curle closed the Whitefield Road boiler shop as Kelvinhaugh Street was on short time. Bow McLachlan shut down never to re-open. Charles Connal and D & W Henderson were closed but would re-open when business picked up. Lobnitz, Simons, Fleming & Ferguson, Ferguson Bros. and A. J. Inglis were all staggering from one crisis to another. Big firms like Fairfields, Harland and Wolff, John Browns, Dennys and Stephens were stumbling along mostly on short time. Beardmore's Parkhead Forge and their Dalmuir Shipyard were in a similar position but they started diversifying, building cars, taxis, commercial vehicles, airships (they built the famous R34) and railway locomotives. Yarrows were still working away but rarely gave Kerr work. The Machine Tool industry of Johnstone was dead as were most of the ancillary manufacturers.

END OF AN ERA

T. C. Kerr fell ill at the end of 1931 at his home at Nettlehurst near Beith in North Ayrshire where he lived with his wife, son and three daughters. On the 24th January 1932 he died leaving chaos behind him. The long slump had taken toll of the firm. Many of their customers had closed down never to re-open. Bob Kerr, T. C. Kerr's brother although not a shareholder had taken on the management from T. C's son David, who had worked in the office. Bob discovered that little capital remained to run the firm. Approaching Mr McIntosh the managing director of the Road Steam Engine Co. Ltd., who were also in severe straits it was agreed to merge the two firms.

FIRMS AMALGAMATE

It was decided to scrap the Thomsons, sell the Aveling and one McLaren, close the Tunnel Street yard and the Scotland Street yard, close the Finnieston office of Road Steam Engine Co. and move the office girl over to Greenbank Street now renamed Marine Street. All the equipment that was required was also moved into Marine Street.

The new company was named Road Engines & Kerr (Haulage) Ltd.

THE COULSON INTERLUDE

It may seem strange that Coulson & Co. of Park Royal, London should come into a history of heavy haulage in Scotland, but they do.

In the early 1920's the Scottish Office formed The Hydro Electric Board to harness some of the vast amount of water power going to waste in the North of Scotland. One of the first big developments was to pipe water from Loch Ericht down to Loch Rannoch, a drop of approximately one thousand feet. A turbine station to generate electricity was built alongside Loch Rannoch's north shore, approximately ten miles from Rannoch Station, a lonely halt on the West Highland Railway.

As well as generators, transformers weighing 75 tons each were required. The contract to supply the generators and transformers was won by the British Thomson Houston Co. Ltd., of Rugby who approached Messrs Coulson to deliver them.

HIGHLAND ROADS

At this time it has to be remembered that road conditions outside towns and cities were poor, especially in the Highlands. The road from the power station to Rannoch Station was a single track with passing places — to allow ordinary vehicles to pass one another. The ground was very soft in places, the road being built over a moss with outcrops of rock, but mainly moss; also numerous streams had to be bridged. When Coulsons manager surveyed the road little did he know what a nightmare the job would become. It was decided to send the transformers by rail to Rannoch Station then transfer them to the road vehicles for the last ten miles.

The railway companies carried the transformers on two H beams slung between two rail wagons. Coulsons decided to do the same, an eight wheeled solid iron-wheeled trailer with turning lock was used to carry the front end of the beam and a six wheeled trailer fitted with manual steering for the rear end of the beams. Those vehicles and the beams were despatched by rail ahead of the first transformer. A Fowler 10 NHP road locomotive MT2430 travelled up by road from London up the A1 and the A9 to Pitlochry then from Kinlochrannoch to Rannoch Station — the end of the road. If there had been no station there would have been no road. To assist the Fowler another local Fowler was hired, registration No. ES 4310 an 8 NHP.

TEN MILES IN THREE WEEKS

In the spring of 1930 the movement commenced. When transferring the load from the rail wagons to Coulsons trailers, the trailer wheels had to sit on steel plates. Three weeks and ten miles later they were still on steel plates. Every inch of the road had to be plated.

Plating meant laying plates end to end in front of the trailer wheels. When cleared they were lifted by hand and loaded on to a two wheeled cart for transportation to the front of the trailer to be laid again. Even with the plates, it was touch and go whether the road would carry the weight on many occasions. Even with all the bridges shored up, the road still required the plates. Coulson's Fowler also had to winch the trailers along using its wire rope through a return block on the drawbar to the rear coupling on the Fowler. The hired traction engine acting as an anchor in front. The traction engines had a winch drum inside the near side rear wheel which could be brought into action by withdrawing two pins from the hub. The transformers and generators were in position by the autumn and the equipment returned to London.

LOCH TUMMEL POWER STATION

In November 1934 they returned to the Highlands as the Tummel power station was ready to receive the heavy equipment again supplied by British Thomson Houston of Rugby. This time Struan station

Continued on page 38.

34. — Coulson & Co. Ltd., of Park Royal, London after loading 75 tons transformer at Rannoch Station, Fowler MT2430 (still in existance and owned by K. Frost of Norwich) and a local hired Fowler 1930. Winching load over plates.

35. — Now making an attempt to haul the load near the Moor of Rannoch Hotel.

36. — A halt while transferring the steel plates from the rear to the front for relaying.
Note the hand steering wheel at the back of the rear bogie to steer it while travelling.

37. — Three weeks later and nearing journeys end — Rannoch Power Station 1930.

38. — 27/11/32 Moving 70 ton stator from Struan Station to Tummel Power Station.
Two extra road locomotives help the original Fowler.

39. — Even with three big road locomotives they are back to plating and winching on the hills, 1932.

40. — Now it's pull and push with stator. Note the back steerer on the trailer.

41. — A close up to the back steering position.

on the Inverness line was used, twelve miles from Tummel Bridge. Three engines travelled north, Fowlers No. 14861 Reg. No. MH5876 and No. 14871 Reg. No. YK1046 joined MT2430. As this time they were not on the Rannoch Moor it was presumed that the three road locomotives would be able to haul even the heaviest load. Unfortunately they still required to plate certain parts of the road and even with the three locos they had to winch all the loads up two hills. It would appear that they moved seven loads between 60 and 80 tons to Tummel. They also moved a 75 ton transformer from Abernethy to Newburgh in Fife before returning home.

THE NEW COMPANY

The management of Road Engines & Kerr (Haulage) Ltd., consisted of R. Kerr, Managing Director, George Mathers, Manager (R. Kerr's son-in-law) and Mr. McIntosh, Director. The engines retained were the two Burrells *Clyde* and *Lord Roberts*, three McLarens No. 1594, 1600 and 1627, one Fowler No. 11271 and one Foden 5 ton wagon No. 7932. So started June 1932.

Mr Bob Kerr approached the Grampian Hydro-Electric Board at their headquarters in Edinburgh for a share of the transformer and heavy machinery movement then being done by Messrs. Coulson. At a Directors meeting, Kerr claimed that they could do the work quicker and more cheaply as their plant was based in Glasgow. As a result a thirty ton and several 40 to 50 ton transformers were moved in 1932/33 while Coulson was still engaged in moving heavy lifts in the Tummel area. The first 75 ton transformer Kerr moved was from Abernethy to Newburgh a distance of five miles, in three hours. Most heavy transformers were moved from the manufacturer by rail to the siding nearest to the site. The heavy haulage contractors jacked it up while the carrying beams were removed, placed on timber beams and rails to slide it over on to the trailer. It would then be hauled to the site to be placed on the plinth, again being jacked up and slid over.

LOCOMOTIVE INDUSTRY

The amalgamation of the two firms provided some work in addition to the transformer movements The railway locomotive industry was also slowly starting to pick up again. A second-hand petrol driven 45 ton articulated Scammell low-loader was purchased in 1933 and the 5 ton Foden scrapped. One of the McLaren engines was put off the road to be used for spares. Later another second-hand Scammell tractor was added to the fleet. These machines could assist the engines to move the steam navvies which were now gaining popularity in the construction industry.

About this time Messrs. Pickford, who were a wholly owned subsidary of Hayes Wharf Cartage of Tooley Street, London and who in turn was partly

42. — Uplifting water at the Falls of Gaur 1934. Once more on the Moor of Rannoch.

43. — Road Engines & Kerr (Haulage) Ltd., ''Clyde'' wire roping a transformer from a railway wagon on to an extending low loading trailer at Perth Harbour.

44. — ''Clyde'' with transformer now en-route to substation, 31/8/33.

owned by the L.M.S. and the L.N.E. Railways, was becoming interested in acquiring various firms of heavy haulage contractors. In 1930 they purchased the company of Norman E Box of Manchester. Robert Kerr, seeing the set-up with Box gradually losing its identity, did not want any dealings with Pickford. Knowing that capital would be required to equip the firm with modern trailers for transformer haulage and other long distance work, he kept his ears open for suggestions. The L.M.S. Railway Company also had shares in a large number of haulage firms including Wordie & Company of Glasgow, who in turn had been buying up various firms in Scotland and North East England. In late 1936 Wordie & Co. started negotiations with a view to buying the business of Road Engines & Kerr (Haulage) Ltd.

WORDIE & COMPANY TAKE OVER

An agreement was reached early in 1937 and Wordie & Co became the owners. Both R Kerr and G Mathers kept their same jobs and the firm retained its name. All employees were paid off by Kerr and restarted by the new company. One of the conditions of sale had been that the name be retained and that the firm would not come under Pickfords jurisdiction.

NEW REGULATIONS

The 1933 Road Traffic Act brought changes to all forms of transport including heavy haulage. The Government now required brakes fitted to trailers and not one of the old Kerrs or Road Engines trailers had brakes. Since 1934 the firm had tried to modify some trailers with wooden blocks pressing against the tyres. It looked good but did not have much effect for usually by the time the flagman had screwed the brakes on the danger was passed.

So new trailers were a necessity. The first was ordered from R. A. Dyson of Liverpool — a flat 60 ton with brakes and oscillating axles, the rear double axle in tandem and four in line on the steering lock. A new 45 ton petrol Scammell unit with a Dyson low-loading trailer arrived shortly afterwards. Another McLaren and the Fowler were withdrawn from service.

In 1937 a new 75 ton trailer was ordered from Dyson, crank-framed with two rows of four double wheels on oscillating axles fitted with screw brakes, and four double wheels on oscillating axles on the steering fore-carriage. It was also decided to purchase two second hand engines, a Fowler 10 NHP No. 9986 Reg. No. NL1028, from Mutter Howey of Newcastle and a McLaren 10 NHP Reg. No. 1650 Reg. No. EB4903 — *Wharfdale Terrier* from a London firm.

The Empire Exhibition in Bellahouston Park, Glasgow provided a lot of work to both John Young and Kerr and industry was busier than it had been for many years.

A number of firms were buying new equipment including Lancashire boilers. In 1939 just before the war started, two ERF diesel articulated units were purchased along with a 45 ton diesel Scammell articulated unit with a 50 ton low loading trailer by Dyson. *Continued on page 45.*

Continued on page 45.

45. — McLaren with Bouldon wheels originally fitted with wooden blocks instead of rubber tyres uncoupled from trailer loaded with paper roller 1934.

46. — A newcomer appears on the scene. 45 ton petrol Scammell 80 BHP with a 30 tons diesel marine engine, 1935.

47. — "Lord Roberts" on nightshift with a six cylinder diesel being traced by a McLaren. George Mathers who eventually took command of the firm is on the left, also in the line are John McNeil, flagman, Ronald Bell sometimes flagman, steerer and later erection foreman and Bob Caldwell engine driver, 1935.

48. — McLaren tracing 45 ton Scammell with a 40 ton transformer from Struan Station to Tummel power scheme. Bridge in photo passes under railway and over river at the same time.

49. — Now halfway up a mountain road as the engine driver oils the motion.

50. — With "Clyde" running empty behind the McLaren hauls the 40 ton transformer with Bob Watson walking alongside as flagman. He later became outside manager.

51. — Stopping on a shored up bridge to pick up water.

52. — Trouble as road sinks and transformer keels over. "Quick! In with timbers and jacks."

53. — "Clyde stands by with wire rope out ready to winch the trailer out of the hole. Ronald Bell ready to signal the driver when Bob Kerr gives the word.

54. — Journeys end with transformer being lowered on to rail bogie to be run into the sub station. 1935/6 for the North of Scotland Hydro Electric Board.

The second world war was to change R. E. & Kerr's whole pattern of work from a local firm to one mainly hauling long distance. Nationally the heavy haulage industry was pooled throughout the country with the exception of Kerr's who came under control of the British Admiralty and under the command of Rear Admiral White based at the St. Enoch Station Hotel Glasgow. All Kerr's drivers and outside foremen had Admiral White's personal telephone number to be consulted in case of difficulty. Long distance work was not entirely new to Kerr's. They had moved the heavy machinery from Coatbridge to Corby for Messrs Stewart & Lloyds in the early thirties and undertaken other work in England and Wales.

Strange to relate because of the tie-up with the Admiralty, the Ministry of War Transport in Glasgow was starved of heavy low-loaders. The M.O.W.T. authorised the purchase of two 45 ton Scammells and a 32 wheeled crane platform trailer with a capacity of 120 tons to Isaac Barrie along with two 80 ton Pioneer Scammell tractors. Also a 50 ton diesel articulated Foden arrived early 1940 to R. E. & Kerr.

COASTAL DEFENCES

After the start of hostilities one ERF was working on coast defence carrying excavators from site to site along the north east coast of Scotland and later in the year around the north coast. The other ERF was moving transformers up to 20 tons between the makers

Continued on page 54.

55. — Isaac Barrie of Glasgow two Sentinel steam wagons No. 5593 Reg No. GB6578 and No. 5887 Reg No. GB7861 with monkeys carrying pressure columns for Babcock & Wilcox Ltd., 1936.

56. — "Lord Roberts" with a land built boat "Carrick Lass" going to be launched at Plantation Quay. Usually these moves were made on a Sunday morning before trams commenced. Taken at Govan Cross 1936.

57. — A McLaren with another boat in Summerton Road en-route to be launched note lifting beams lashed to the hull.

58. — A Scammell with a 42 tons cheek for a rolling mill from Beardmores of Parkhead.

59. — A McLaren with a set of Triple expansion cylinders for a large steam engine, 1936.

60. — Wee man looking up at an 80 ton boiler for the S.S. Clan Campbell hauled by ''Lord Roberts'' on the ''Loch Ness Monster'' trailer weighing 36 tons empty. Five boilers were required this being the first, 20/1/1937.

61. — The second ''Clan Campbell'' 80 ton boiler being lifted by the hammerhead crane in James Watt Dock, Greenock. ''Lord Robert's'' on the job 1937.

62. — This petrol engined Scammell tractor, later converted to diesel when a five cylinder Gardner was fitted, has a load of two combustion chambers for economy boilers. The boilers themselves were carried on other vehicles.

48

63. — "Clyde" and a 45 ton Scammell each with an economy boiler approx 35 tons after loading in
Wilsons of Lilybank off London Road, Glasgow, 1937.

64. — Lined up ready to leave for Nottingham. The route taken was to Edinburgh down the A1 via Newcastle Upon Tyne.
The boilers were there erected by Kerrs men at Nottingham Co-operative Society.

65. — A John G. Kincaids diesel being lifted off a Road Engines & Kerr trailer
in the Victoria Harbour, Greenock 1937.

66. — Delivering the Tobermory Life Boat into the Empire Exhibition, Glasgow 1938.
A McLaren with new Dyson flat 60 ton trailer.

67. — McLaren with a David Rowan 80 ton boiler going to the Finnieston 130 ton crane Glasgow, 1938.

68. — "Clyde" with 50 ton half diesel bedplate for Harland & Wolff, Glasgow from their own foundry in Helen Steet, 1938. Bedplate was able to be delivered by "Clyde" alone as the trailer ran on ballraces.

69. — First of a new breed. Equipped with a 6LW Gardner diesel engine is the 45 ton Scammell.
Here with a Dyson 50 ton trailer carrying a 42 ton cheek for a rolling mill from Beardmores, Glasgow 1939.

70. — Loading a New Zealand railway locomotive in Hydepark works on double trailers 1938/39.

71. — Leaving the works with one engine back shoving. Forty locomotives were ordered and delivered before the outbreak of war. Date of order 29/9/38.

72. — R. E. Kerrs ERF with a Drysdale of Yoker pump 1941/42.

73. — Wartime scene at Stobcross 175 ton electric crane with "Clan Campbell" loading a barge. In the foreground old solid iron wheeled bogies, one with a marine boiler awaiting its turn at the crane. Early 1940's.

Bruce Peebles of Edinburgh and sub-stations all over Scotland. The other vehicles carried on with the normal day to day traffic.

Clyde and a McLaren G6804 with a coal wagon and living van journeyed to Liverpool to pick up another new 75 ton trailer from Dyson. The construction of this trailer was actually sub-contracted by Dysons to Cranes of Dereham who had heavier manufacturing capacity. Pickfords of Manchester had a 70 ton transformer lying at the builders Metro Vickers to go to a sub-station at Motherwell. The transformer, after being loaded on the new trailer, travelled to Kendal where the other McLaren EB4903 met them for the long haul over Shap.

On the road south Clyde's driver, Wattie Muir, coming over Shap for the first time in his life and in fog, did not see how steep the gradient was and told Bob Kerr on the phone that he would not require a third engine. But Pickfords manager had been adamant and Wattie was greatly relieved to see George Tough with the extra McLaren when he saw the gradient on Shap the next day.

A TORTUOUS ROUTE

Early in 1940 Kerr was asked to move two 60 ton boilers from David Rowan in Glasgow to Hall Russell of Aberdeen. Normally this traffic moved by puffer through the Forth and Clyde Canal then up the East Coast, but hit and run raiders had stopped the small coasters. The road was surveyed by Robert Kerr and the proposed route approved by local authorities then passed to Admiral White for his approval. The first boiler was hauled by *Clyde*, a McLaren EB4903 and a Scammell tractor.

Travelling via Stirling, making a detour of one mile to Bridge of Allan because of a low bridge on the main road; main road to Greenloaning; detour via Crieff because of a low bridge in Perth, then entering Perth from the other side, Dundee, Kingsway. Making for Arbroath they ran into real trouble. They could not get passed a road block for the threatened invasion and the local policeman refused to let them pull it down. Wattie Muir phoned Rear Admiral White. An hour later a 5 ton Bedford arrived with a squad of naval ratings and an Officer in charge. The Officer ordered his men to remove the obstruction with picks and crowbars from the truck while the policeman protested to no avail. On they went to Arbroath, detoured Inverkeillor to avoid a low bridge. At Stonehaven a further detour via the Slug Road added another 16 miles before Aberdeen eventually was reached. After this the roads under some of the bridges were lowered to save such time wasting detours.

A 45 ton Scammell was on loan to the Royal Tank Corps as a tank transporter, being used to train crews on loading and unloading tanks on Rannoch Moor. *Lord Roberts* spent most of the time in Greenock, occasionally calling for assistance with heavy loads, just as another engine had been during the first world war. The firms in Greenock and Port Glasgow were J. G. Kincaid, and Rankin & Blackmore, both boilermakers and engine builders and the shipyards were Lithgows, George Brown, Scotts and Ferguson Bros. Boilers were delivered to Leith, Burntisland, Troon and Dundee and engines were delivered to Burntisland, Troon, Dundee, Wallsend and Peterhead, sternframes and rudders to Birkenhead, Newcastle, Sunderland, Havertonhill, Dundee and Southampton. Machinery of various kinds went to Salford dock, Liverpool, Middlesborough, Nottingham and Bedford, coming back into Scotland from the South with a variety of traffic and ship engines for Leith and Greenock.

HYDRO BOARD INSTALLATIONS

An order was received to move a 75 ton transformer from Struan Station to Tummel. The 75 ton transformer was transported from The British Thompson Houston Co. Ltd., Rugby by rail to Struan then transferred to Pickford's 32-wheeled crane bogie, borrowed for the job. *Clyde* with driver Wattie Muir was traced by McLaren EB4903 and a Scammell tractor with the green McLaren G6804 standing by. It took seven hours running time for the 12 miles with a modern trailer against Coulsons three weeks with iron wheeled bogies ten years previously. Snow caused the trailer to be left at Tummel for three months but the traction engines arrived home.

Early in 1941 another 75 ton transformer was moved from Nethybridge to Boat of Garten using one of Kerr's trailers. At this period transformers in sub stations were being upgraded. For instance, a 20 tonner would be put in, and a 18 tonner taken out to another sub station, then a 16 out and so on until only a little one was left with the Hydro Board. Diesel articulated vehicles spent weeks changing them over.

The Clydebank Blitz on 13/14th March 1941

74. — A wartime built 45 ton Scammell delivered 1942. Loaded with part of rudder bracket for a large aircraft carrier being built at Cammell Lairds of Birkenhead. Cast at the Steel Company of Scotland, Hallside near Cambuslang 1945. Note the masked head lamps and the all-welded trailer which was one of the first produced by Scammell Lorries Ltd.

was followed by the Greenock Blitz in May of the same year. Greenock Power Station, situated right in the centre of the town escaped serious damage until the last of the five nights of the blitz. A piece of shrapnel punctured the bottom of an 80 ton transformer allowing the cooling oil to run out, setting it on fire and causing a chain re-action throughout the whole power station.

At Kippen Railway Station the Electricity Department had a secret store for transformers and other large generating equipment. Away from towns and the industrial belt it was serviced by a railway line right into the 100 ton crane in the building. When Kerr's vehicles arrived on the scene the drivers were instructed to remove the mask from the offside head light and insert a disc with the magic letters RP/E — Road Priority — Electricity. An eighty ton transformer was loaded on a big Dyson trailer with *Clyde* , a McLaren G6804 and assisted by ALH363 Scammell tractor.

Leaving about 12 noon they ran to the Whins of Milton — about 12 miles, then on the second day to Muirhead — about 15 miles, through Glasgow to Davieland Road in Whitecraigs on the third day, then a good run to Kilwinning via Kilmarnock and Irvine. But on the fifth day between Inverkip and Greenock the road collapsed on a hastily filled bomb crater and the trailer went down to sit on the main beams. It took two days jacking for a foundation and four days to get it out. When delivered, the McLaren winched it off the trailer while *Clyde* pulled down a dangerous building damaged by the bombing.

MOVING A GIANT PRESS

Ayr Stampworks had the largest press in Scotland on order and Kerr's had the job of transporting the anvil block in three pieces. The base of the anvil weighed 130 tons, placed on top of it was a 119 ton piece, then on top of this was the smallest piece — a mere 99 tons. *Clyde* with the two McLarens moved the largest piece first, spread between two trailers coupled back to back as the road was very soft in places. The anvil blocks were transported by rail to Auchincruive Station four miles from the works. Kerr's outside squad under foreman James Barnes jacked it up and slid it across on to the double trailers. On reaching the works it was again jacked up and slid on to the top of railway sleepers which had been crows-nested (criss-crossed) inside the pit which was to hold the complete anvil. Jacks capable of lifting 100 tons were borrowed from Sir William Arrol Ltd., which were lower than Kerr's own, to avoid undue sway in the pit. It took six weeks of jacking (removing three inches at a lift at each end) to position the anvil block at the bottom of the pit. The other two pieces were handled more quickly as they had not to be lowered so far. As this and other jobs were tying up men for a considerable time, four more experienced men were started, men used to working with showground engines.

WAR WORK

One ERF was employed every third week delivering an 18 ton set of diesel engines shipped over by Burns Laird cargo boat from Harland & Wolff of Belfast to the Clydevilla crane. These went in turn to

Buckie, Fraserburgh and Peterhead, where four boatyards were turning out wooden hulled minesweepers.

James Kerr and his squad were placing machines into position in gun factories, just as they had been doing during the first world war. Of course they were all a good age by this time and indeed if it had not been for the war, James and his squad would have been retired.

A third outside squad with Bob Watson, in charge was erecting all the heavy machinery and tanks at the I.C.I. Ltd., factories in Dumfries, Powfoot, Dalbeattie and later at Girvan.

In 1941 number four outside squad with Ronald Bell in charge were erecting machinery in MacConnachies Canning Factory in Fraserburgh when a Nazi hit-and-run raider bombed and machine gunned the factory killing seventeen girls.

I REMEMBER IT WELL.....

An E.R.F. returning to Glasgow from Fraserburgh came upon one of the ex showmen, Herbie Knowles standing in the middle of the moor at Carnbo near Milnathort, Kinross-shire. The E.R.F. stopped, the secondman asked him if he was waiting for a bus. His reply was "No! I am guarding a crankshaft". Well, nothing resembling a crankshaft was in sight, in fact there was nothing except the moor in sight. "That rag on the fence marks the spot where the 50 ton crankshaft lies and if it's moved, the crankshaft is lost" was the expanation given by Herbie. Watty Muir who had been 'Clyde's' normal driver was ill and Bert Kilvington who normally drove the 'Lord Roberts' replaced Watty. But Bert was not familiar with the road to Dundee. On passing over the moor he had pulled into the offside of the road to lift water from a small stream, not knowing that the road was laid on moss. On pulling in, the offside tandem wheels sunk into the road and the crankshaft slid off the trailer breaking the holding wires like thread. Within seconds the crankshaft sank out of sight.

Bob Watson and his squad were re-directed to Carnbo along with the E.R.F. and a load of jacks, round plates, H beams, wires and wooden wedges to join up with the McLaren EB4903 and two living vans. It took two weeks of jacking, up to their thighs in water, using H beams lashed across the throws of the crankshaft as jacking pads. Once foundation was reached, it took another week to get it out. The plates and timber used for the foundation are still there to day.

Then the crankshaft was split, a five ton piece loaded on the E.R.F. and the 45 ton remainder loaded on to a 45 ton Scammell for the return to Greenock. There it was found to be not a thousand of an inch out despite all this handling.

In May 1942, Robert Kerr journeyed to South Wales to meet and buy two engines from Mrs Deakin of Showland. A 10 NHP Fowler No. 20223, named *Supreme* and an 8 NHP Burrell No. 4092, named *Simplicity* the last Burrell built, arrived a few weeks later to have their dynamoes, plates, curly brass and chrome removed and their canopies shortened with heavier couplings built on the rear.

In that year too, sadly the *Lord Roberts,* Fowler No. 9986 were scrapped along with two old Scammells and later the McLaren G6804. One new Scammell tractor and an articulated 45 tonner arrived as replacements.

WAGON ARRESTED

At this time excavators were in short supply. John Young & Co. picked up a Ruston Bucyrus dragline from Peterhead and journeyed down to County Durham before being stopped by the Police. The driver and mate were put up in a local hotel and the wagon "arrested" while The Admiralty and Ministry of Aircraft Production fought for control of the dragline. Three days elapsed then they returned to Peterhead. The Admiralty won.

PREPARING FOR THE INVASION

Quadruple expansion engines weighing 66 tons for Corvettes were being built all over the country and had to be transported in two pieces. Bedplate, crankshaft and columns weighing 42 tons and the cylinders weighing 24 tons. That is until John Young built a trailer to suit the job enabling them to be shifted in one piece. Of course he could not move them all.

An E.R.F. 20 ton articulated low loader carried an 18 ton boiler from Andersons of Carfin, Lanarkshire to Richard Dunston's of Thorne near Doncaster every week for about two years, these boilers were part of the propulsion machinery of tugboats being built for the Normandy invasion. Invasion barges were being put together in boiler shops, garages, pieces of waste land, as well as dock yards and boat yards. They all had to be moved to the nearest river or the trailer reversed into the sea. In the midst of all this, normal traffic still moved around the Clydeside. Ship boilers were being overproduced and were left lying on waste land until hulls could be built for them. In 1943 the British Admiralty asked Kerr's to move a number of ships boilers from Clarks of Sunderland to a piece of waste land a quarter of a mile away. To do this *Clyde*, a McLaren EB4903 and a Scammell tractor left Glasgow with an 80 ton excavator for Blyth then picked up a 100 ton excavator from Newcastle Town Moor to Crook in County Durham before reporting to Sunderland. The road rose steeply from the quayside up to the piece of ground chosen to store the boilers, so steeply that both engines had to use their maximum power by injecting live steam into both cylinders to keep the boiler moving. Four boilers were moved in this way. Then the engines loaded a 42 ton load for Leith on the way home.

Several big loads were still being moved by traction engines. A big rudder from Beardmores in Parkhead, Glasgow, 25 feet wide, was delivered to Newcastle via Berwick-on-Tweed. It was too wide to get through the Old Wall Gate at Berwick and had to detour to Coldstream then back to Tweedmouth — one mile away from Berwick and taking eleven hours. The crews stayed in the same lodgings for two nights in succession.

75. — Albion gun tractor owned by the British Admiralty, one of the two on loan to R. E. Kerr to replace the "Lord Roberts" and two McLarens. Turning into Dock Street in Dundee with 108 ton half bedplate and crankshaft for a diesel supplied by J. G. Kincaid for Caledon Shipyard, Dundee. Carried on a 75 ton Dyson trailer and back shoved by a 45 ton wartime Scammell tractor. Late 1945 from Greenock to Dundee three days running time. A distance of 100 miles.

PRACTICALLY SPEAKING

One day in the spring of 1943 I was sent out to assist 'Clyde' and EB4903 McLaren No. 1650 10 NHP, 'Wharfdale Terrier' in unloading a huge ship's boiler off the trailer on to round plates by the roadside. This was the scene: 'Clyde's' rope was over the top of the boiler to hold it back when it dropped the 22 inches off the trailer. The McLaren's wire rope was reeved through a snatch block shackled on to the side of the trailer to pull the boiler down and off the trailer. The McLaren was standing on the road behind the trailer. The reason for this activity was a bridge with only sixteen feet clearance which was too low to allow the load through on its journey to Edinburgh.

The Glasgow to Edinburgh road in those days comprised of a three lane carriageway about thirty feet wide with the same width again in grass stretching from Carntyne to Corstorphine, a distance of forty miles. Approximately fifteen miles of this grass verge was occupied with cased Hurricane fighters awaiting shipment to the various war zones.

Fortunately for us the bridge was well clear of the cases. The boiler was dropped on to three-feet diameter by half-inch thick steel plates and when the trailer was pulled clear by the McLaren, 'Clyde' slewed the boiler round into position to be rolled under the bridge. Normally marine boilers were loaded complete with smoke box but this boiler had nothing attached to it as the builders knew that it would have to be roped through the bridges en route. When 'Clyde' cleared the road, a Lanarkshire County Council Aveling tractor passed with the whistle blaring and the driver nearly falling off the footplate waving to us.

Certain boiler makers built for certain engine builders who did not have a boiler shop of their own. This was the case in this instance. Henry Robb of Leith were old customers of Barclay Curle. Before the war a puffer would have sailed through the Forth and Clyde Canal with one boiler at a time without any fuss but owing to the war puffers were in short supply we lifted the plates when the boiler cleared them and relayed them in front of the boiler as 'Clyde's' wire rolled the boiler under the bridge. Once clear of the structure the wire was shifted to slew the boiler into loading position. Meanwhile George Tough the McLaren's driver boiled the teacans to save time before blocking the road again when loading. Although the Police had been informed we never saw them. This was probably just as well as we worked things to suit ourselves. After twenty minutes break the trailer was backed into position by the McLaren and 'Clyde' moved alongside the trailer in line with the boiler. The McLaren then uncoupled and a road was plated around the boiler where she could hold the boiler back when dropping into the space between the channels of the trailer. Twelve-inch blocks about five feet long were placed longways between the boiler and trailer. Then a six-inch thick timber about three feet long placed longways on top of the twelve -inch blocks with one end against the trailer. A three inch piece two feet long was put on top to feed the boiler on to the trailer, otherwise 'Clyde' would have had a dead lift.

With the boiler safely on board, we had just finished loading the plates and timbers on to the coal trailer when the rain came on. As we started climbing up towards Newhouse through a nineteen feet high overhead bridge, sleet, then snow fell. Fortunately, it melted on the road but it was uncomfortable riding the trailer. Hurricane lamps were lit and it was dark when we pulled into the disused old road to park for the night at Newhouse. This was the second night out, the first had been at the Glasgow end of the Edinburgh road, five miles from the boiler shop through the city traffic. Now we were fifteen miles from Glasgow. We took the bus into Glasgow arriving at 7.30 pm in pouring rain. Arrangements were made to get the first bus at 8.00 am as it was a two hourly service. (God help anyone who missed it).

Next morning I met Watty Muir, 'Clyde's' driver, on the tram into town, nodded then sat apart as protocol demanded that Watty sat with his steerer, Tammy Fleming. We arrived forty five minutes before the bus turned up at the bus terminus on riverside. There was no shelter as rain continued to pour down. Watty counted our men, twice, before Will Hardy, the McLaren's steerer, ambled up. Before arriving at Newhouse we sat freezing on the bus as it wandered round half of Lanarkshire. As I was spare man I refilled the oil lamps as the engine crews prepared for the road. The rain had turned to sleet as we pulled out to continue our journey. I passed time counting the aircraft boxes as we rolled along the few miles to our next bridge in Harthill. Watty decided to let us have a drink of tea before unloading the boiler. We were now on a bus route with one bus in each direction every hour. We had to time the road-blocking not to hold up the service buses. By this time the snow was blowing horizontally in pellets and it was five hours later before we had the boiler unloaded and reloaded. In all that time we never saw one of the locals — only an occasional lorry, forbye the buses

The load was pulled forward about fifty feet with red lamps placed around it for the night. When a Wordie & Co. wagon appeared through the snow with half a load on it, Watty, Tammy and Will squeezed into the cab and the rest of us climbed on the back to sit in the snow, all the way back to Glasgow. But it was still quicker than the bus.

Monday morning 7.00 am saw us on the bus to Harthill. The rain and snow had ceased along with the wind, instead it was a nice fresh frosty morning. Once the lamps were collected and refilled, we proceeded the ten miles to Pumpherston Road End for the last low

bridge. There was a bit of a mystery about this route we had to take. The normal heavy haulage route from Harthill to Edinburgh was via the Calders with no low bridges or obstructions and here we were still on the main road with a low bridge ahead. The job appeared to go twice as quickly as the previous day's even with the increase in traffic and our finger tips raw with the cold and wet when handling the plates.

We ran into Newbridge and parked for the night as we had to turn off the main road about a mile ahead to get on to the original route again via Saughton where the tram wires had to be lifted all the way to Leith. We bussed back that night to Glasgow on a more direct bus route and were back on the first bus from Glasgow at 5.30 am the next morning arriving at Newbridge at 7.00 am.

I have no idea how they completed the journey through Edinburgh as while we waited outside the prison for the wire lifters a 45 ton Scammell caught up with us. Harry Fleming, old Tammy's son, who was the driver, jumped out of the cab to inform me that I had to go at once with him to Wallsend with a load from Leith dock — this meant being away for eight days without soap, towel or anything. Such was heavy haulage in those days.

War production continued unabated. Boilers went to Burntisland, Dundee and Aberdeen. Arrester gears for stopping planes on aerodromes, similar to those on aircraft carriers were being constructed at Coatbridge and delivered all over Eastern England. Four point five inch twin-turret guns were being constructed at Vickers in Newcastle for ships being built in Glasgow — at 45 tons each they were moved by Scammells.

LOADING AT A LEVEL CROSSING

Stern and rudder frames were being cast at Beardmores, the Steel Company of Scotland at Hallside near Cambuslang and prefabricated at Colvilles of Glengarnock in North Ayrshire. Where the road out of the works was too narrow to allow the big frames to come out, they had to be loaded by two steam railway cranes at a level crossing in the village Main Street after the local bus went by. The whole population turned out for this spectacle.

ENGINES BUILT ON TRAILER

At Ferguson Brothers in Port Glasgow the overhead crane in the fitting shop could not lift the finished engines so Kerr ran an empty trailer in three days before the engines were due to leave the works and they erected the engines on the trailer. When leaving the works each of Kerr's men were presented with a shilling (5p) by one of the brothers to hansel the set of engines.

Rankin & Blackmore built 60 ton boilers and marine engines halfway up a hill in Greenock on the wrong side of a 12 foot high bridge. This firm was the builders of the paddle steamer "Waverley's" propulsion machinery.

Here are a few incidents which were all part of the regular day to day scene. Kerr borrowed a Pickfords 32 wheeled crane trailer for a steam accumulator to be transported from Annan to Blochairn Steelworks, Glasgow, a distance of approximately 93 miles. Similar to the one moved before the war to Beckton Gas Works. It travelled via Lanark, Carluke and Motherwell.

A rail locomotive boiler stuck when being loaded into the 'tween decks of a cargo ship. The driver and his mate jacked it out.

An excavator stuck in Loch Fyne by the tide and half covered by sand was rescued by an E.R.F. crew with very little tackle while the army went about its business all around with recovery vehicles fitted with the latest equipment. It was quite simply done, a pound sterling was offered to a sergeant in charge of a big Scammell with a winch to go to the canteen for tea and to leave his vehicle nose into a big tree with the winch pointing to the excavator. Pulling the wire out as far as it would go, then add Kerr's wires coupled on to the nearest solid part of the base. After lashing the Scammell to the tree as an anchor, the winch took the strain, everything tightened up then out she came, out of the sand. Halting only to shorten the wire, she was on the trailer before the Scammell crew returned from the canteen. A Scammell tractor without a winch but with a 250 fathom wire, with two and three reeve blocks recovered a barge from a sand bank in Gareloch.

Portable boilers on iron wheels were moved around the docks to supply steam to Naval ships in for refitting.

MAIN A1 BRIDGE COLLAPSES

In May 1944 a cheek for a rolling mill (cheeks are the uprights that hold the rollers) was despatched from Beardmores of Parkhead for Robertsons of Bedford. This was a rough casting weighing 60 tons. At Robertsons it was machined to fit a mill in Falkirk. Kerr carried it down on a Scammell with another tracing. About two months later Pickford had the job of delivering it to Falkirk. It was loaded on to a 100 ton trailer with two Diamond T's (U.S.A. built tractors weighing about 20 tons each) in attendance, one at the front and one back shoving. All went well until arriving in Boroughbridge on the A1 which was the main route from South to North on the eastern side of England. All traffic crossed a stone bridge over a river and canal and as Pickfords front tractor entered the bridge an eight wheeler travelling south, came on, then hesitated and stopped. The tractor driver had been pulling then braked, then pulled again. This started the bridge structure to sway. When the big trailer rolled on to the bridge the additional weight caused the structure to collapse. The trailer landed in the river and the back shover on top of it. The front tractor's front end being up in the air and the back end down. There was consternation all around. Hurried byepasses were put into operation via Thirsk and Tadcaster and it took a long time to sort things out. But as a result of this serious accident a big problem now faced the heavy haulage industry because road authorities throughout the country imposed weight restrictions on nearly every bridge.

———

PORTOBELLO TO SOUTHAMPTON

Fourteen days after D-Day, June 6th 1944, two 45 ton Scammells loaded two 50 ton wreck lifting pontoons from the Engineering Works at Marine Gardens in Portobello which had formerly been a showground and pleasuredrome. Now as well as the pontoons they built landing craft. With a Scammell tractor in attendance they left for Southampton. The overall height was 16 feet and the total weight of each vehicle 67 tons. Because of both the bridge weight restrictions and the height of the load the vehicles were escorted by the police from Portobello to Dalkeith then travelled on their own over Soutra Hill through Lauder to Coldstream and Longframlington. Then it was on to Morpeth with a bridge detour, on to Newcastle and Gateshead, leaving the A1 to Sunderland Houghton le Spring, Stockton into Darlington, Thirsk, byepassing York to Tadcaster and to Doncaster. Continuing on the A1 to Markham Moor a detour was made to the outskirts of Lincoln before swinging back on to the A1, through Newark.

The overhead railway bridge before Grantham caused a real problem, it was 16 feet high the same as the loads. The first load was thought to be too high until one of the attendants climbed on to the bridge then hanging over, guided the load between the rows of rivets on the bridge — giving about an eighth of an inch clearance. The second vehicle approaching when the first was under the bridge and the crew thought from a distance that there was no hope of passing through but once again the almost impossible was achieved. Continuing down through the narrow streets of Stamford to Biggleswade, a police car and motor cyclist were waiting to provide escort around London where at the time, doodle-bugs had a nasty habit of falling out of the sky. From Biggleswade to Camberly was a mystery, it was zig zag all the way except for a six hour delay near Park Royal to change a solid tyre off one of the articulated's driving wheels. Pickford collected the wheel, pressed on a new tyre then returned it. Just past Camberley the Army Military Police took over from the London police as escorts taking them into Southampton which was controlled by the Military. This was the main port supplying the Mulberry harbours and French ports.

Time taken for the journeys was fourteen days travelling plus three days awaiting a crane which only appeared after the crews threatened to unload the pontoons right into the water.

76. — Albion gun tractor, the second one on loan with a 35 ton rudder casting and quadrant from Beardmores of Glasgow to Birkenhead. Loaded on a new Dyson trailer fitted with air brakes. The three men in the photograph from right, the driver John Tough, his brother George Tough who normally drove a McLaren and his steerer W. Hardy. Taken in Liverpool, early 1945.

REPLACING THE STEAM TRACTION ENGINES

Bob Kerr asked Rear Admiral White for two U.S.A. built Diamond T's 6 x 4 tractors. Those machines were heavier than the 80 ton Scammells being built for the army as tank transporters. Pickford had two which were the ideal answer for replacing the steam traction engines which were now becoming obsolete. Unfortunately they were in short supply and instead two Albion 6 x 4 gun tractors, which were experimental at that time, were offered. They were good machines but too light to replace the traction engines as the trailer had the bad habit of shoving them to one side when descending hills with a heavy load.

MINE ON FIRE

An Albion and a Scammell tractor delivered a boiler to Burntisland in Fife. The Scammell was left to return the empty trailer to Glasgow once it had been unloaded. While awaiting the crane a policeman on a push bike arrived to inform the driver of an emergency and that he had to report immediately to the Ministry of Mines open-cast site at Blairingone in Clackmannanshire. Chasing on the crane and before the boiler was right clear of the trailer the Scammell pulled the trailer out into the street. The timbers were sorted and tied on before dashing off at 15 miles per hour to the emergency. On arrival at Blairingone the driver was informed that a pit was on fire at Plean in Stirlingshire. This was about twenty miles away and a 120 ton excavator had to be moved there to isolate the fire. This was to be done by digging down to the effected seam which was about twenty feet below the

77. — "Clyde" delivering a set of rail locomotive frames to the floating crane to join the boiler lying in the bows. All to be transhipped to a cargo ship loading nearby. Late 1944 in Yorkhill basin Glasgow.

surface and allow the miners to work on, as the country was in desperate need of coal. A second tractor was also to assist as the Scammell was only good for 35 tons including the trailer weighing 25 tons. To save weight the dragline jib was removed. This was 120 feet long and weighed about 10 tons, but time did not allow for the A frame to be dismantled.

Loading the excavator on to the trailer, the Scammell set off with one of Aitkens of Linlithgows recovery vehicles, coupled on to the rear to backshove and hold back down a long steep rise that had to be negotiated. A detour was made around by Bridge of Allan because of a 15 foot bridge then into Stirling. There the Kerrs other Albion met up with the Scammell and took over from the Aitken vehicle. (The Aitken driver was glad to leave for home as he did not fancy this sort of job). By this time it was dark and the police said carry on, and provided escort for load, as no lights were available. The Albion and the Scammell double headed the trailer right up to the spot between Plean and Auchenbowie on the main Glasgow to Stirling road, where floodlights had been set up to give light to unload the digger and get it working. The jib was replaced before it was unloaded with all hands assisting. Then the empty trailer was pulled into a field by the Scammel to park for the night. The trailer was backed out at 8.00 am next morning and the scorched wheat was apparent in the field above the fire. By this time the big digger had isolated the fire from the remainder of the pit while the big-hearted miners worked on.   .

THE WAY IT WAS

In October 1944 Messrs John G Kincaid of Greenock had an order for six 60 ton boilers for India and they had to be on the ship in seven days time. Unfortunately the ship was loading in Glasgow. Although it is only twenty two miles from Greenock to Glasgow, the route which had to be taken was via the high Inverkip road to Largs, Ardrossan, Irvine, Kilmarnock, Giffnock, Barrhead Road, Boydstone Road, Cowglen Road, Crookston Road, Paisley Road, Glasgow Bridge to Stobcross crane — a distance of 100 miles — all because of a low bridge.

The race against time began when a Scammell tractor with an empty 75 ton trailer was located in Kincardine-on-Forth by the local policeman, who had been on the lookout. The driver was instructed to proceed immeadiatley to Greenock, where the 75 ton trailer was required, and to be there before 8.00 am on Sunday — it was already 7.00 pm on Saturday night.

It was very unusual to run after dark with large vehicles as the blackout regulations did not allow the trailers to be adequately lit. This practice was hazardous both for the driver and for the other road users. A single masked headlight and two peeps of sidelights on the tractor, one hurricane oil lamp on each side of the front of the trailer and one red hurricane oil lamp at the rear of the trailer was all that was allowed.

Climbing up the long drag from the canal to Cumbernauld the rear hurricane lamp went out. As it could have been fatal to attempt to relight the lamp, it was decided to run on and hope that a cigarette cupped in the driver's hand turned to the rear would warn overtaking drivers to be on their guard. Stopping in Riddrie clear of the main road the lamp was relit for travelling through the City of Glasgow. The second man hung out of the window to warn late night revellers who tended to wander all over the road without seeing the trailer.

Stopping at Kerr's yard a temporary repair was made to the faulty hurricane lamp. Now with a comforting red glow behind they set off on the last twenty-one miles to Victoria Harbour, Greenock to drop the 75 ton trailer. A policeman on duty in the harbour produced a can of tea for the driver and his mate before they left for Glasgow with the Scammell, arriving at Mavisbank at 5.00 am. Three traction engine crews were leaving the yard for Greenock. They were 'Clyde', 'Simplicity' and McLaren EB4903 with two trailers for loading and two coal wagons. At 2.00 pm 'Clyde' traced by the McLaren left Victoria Harbour Greenock with the first boiler. At Inverkip the hurricane lamps were lit and shortly afterwards the McLaren's steerer asked the driver to slow down. The difficulty was that unlike both the Fowler and the Burrell, the McLaren had right hand steering and in the dark the steerer could not see the kerb. Fortunately there was very little traffic and they proceeded at a crawl until Wemyss Bay where they stopped for water. Walter Muir, the leading driver phoned George Mathers, expaining their predicament. George called out an Albion and a Scammell (whose driver had been working since Saturday morning but had managed four hours sleep on Sunday evening before being called out again).

Meeting the engines near Ardrossan, the two diesels took over and made good time. Reaching Barrhead Road at the junction with Boydstone Road at 5.00 in the morning when the road collapsed and the trailer sank owing to a flooded culvert. Admiral White was advised while an outside squad jacked up the trailer and plated it over the soft part of the road. The Renfrew County Council Roads Department were called out and the road was rebuilt before the next boiler arrived, covering the repair with large steel plates for safety. The Albion waited with the load while the Scammell returned to move the locomotive sections frame, boiler and tender from the Atlas to King George V dock at Shieldhall.

At 7.00 am on Monday 'Supreme' and 'Simplicity' left Greenock making Irvine that night, again the Albion and Scammell took over arriving at Stobcross at 5.00 am. 'Supreme' and 'Simplicity' returned to Greenock. 'Supreme' continued to load the boilers and 'Clyde' with 'Simplicity' ran a boiler to Irvine on Wednesday and Friday where the diesels picked them up and delivered them. Meanwhile two Scammells moved two boilers direct from Greenock one on Wednesday night, taking twelve hours for the journey. The last boiler being delivered at 1.00 pm on Saturday when the drivers were congratualted by Rear Admiral White.

During daylight the same vehicles and drivers moved locomotive parts from Queens Park Locomotive Works and, Hydepark and Atlas, all going for shipment.

DIESELS SET TO TAKE OVER

It was now becoming evident that the new breed of diesel tractors were far ahead of the older steam traction engines — particularly for long distance haulage work although they continued to be used for local work where there strength was still unmatched by the diesels of the day.

For example at the end of 1944 *Clyde* travelled down on a 75 ton trailer to move boilers at Clarks of Sunderland assisted by an Albion and a Scammell. Without *Clyde* the boilers would never have been able to be moved up the incline by the diesel engines then available.

Clyde assisted by two Scammells moved a 108 ton excavator from one coal site to another locally then was loaded on to the trailer for return to Glasgow.

The same year an Albion assisted by a Scammell delivered a 90 ton bedplate and crankshaft to Cammel Lairds of Birkenhead. *Clyde* and the McLaren EB4903 journeyed to Newcastle with a 42 ton bedplate then over to Sunderland where they met up with an Albion to move two more boilers at Clarks. This was the last time the McLaren was in England.

THE ALNWICK INCIDENT

An Albion and Scammell delivered a 108 ton part bedplate and crankshaft from Kincaids in Greenock to Dundee being assisted over the Moss at Carnbo by a second Scammell. When moving the same load to the Tyneside the light weight Albion was pushed to one side when descending a steep hill near Ford in Northumberland. Replacing the Albion with another, lower geared, the same thing happened again near Alnwick wheie the load demolished the Duke's boundary wall on his estate. As a result of this incident Kerr lost John G Kincaids of Greenock's work to Isaac Barrie. George Mathers had not informed them of the Alnwick accident with the Albions. It only came out when a picture of the bedplate appeared in a Newcastle Upon Tyne newspaper. Although no damage was done to the load, Kincaids Directors were not pleased.

78. — Fowler "Supreme" traced by Burrell "Simplicity" with a Malaysian locomotive leaving Hydepark works with author walking at side of trailer, 1944.

At the end of the second world war Bob Kerr died after a long illness leaving George Mathers in charge of the business, with Bob Watson as outside manager taking charge of all heavy lifts and erections. Colonel Wordie, Chairman of the holding company realising that Kerr's would require a skilled man to take over within the forseeable future sent a bright young man, Alex MacKinlay, from Wordies Head Office to understudy Mathers.

CLYDE DISAPPEARS

In 1947, the famous Burrell *Clyde* who had served various owners faithfully since 1912 was sold. Some mystery surrounds the circumstances of the sale. *Clyde* was bought by a young showman who drove her down the A74 with his wife steering never to be seen again. Many sightings of *Clyde* have been rumoured in the years since then but all have proved false. The two Albions went back to the Admiralty and were replaced by two Diamond T's, the U.S.A. built tank transporters that Kerr had wanted during the war. Business was brisk with the new transformers replacing the old overworked ones. Locomotives coming out of the works practically every day either in parts or in one piece were being hauled by the last Fowler and Burrell road locomotives left in the fleet and still using the 1926 built *Loch Ness Monster*. Shipbuilding continued as diesel-engined ships were built to replace the old steamers.

79. — Fowler "Supreme" shunting trailer inside Hydepark Works with Egyptian State Railways locomotive on board. Mid 1947.

80. — "Simplicity" and "Supreme" en-route from Hydepark to Stobcross Crane five miles away, 1947.

81. — In Parliamentary Road with a Coronation tram following and a standard tram passing, 1947.

82. — Passing up Sauchiehall Street, Alex MacKinlay looking on.
He later became Pickfords chief heavy lift man in the U.K.

64

83. — 45 ton Scammell with 23 feet high Yarrow boiler at Mavisbank Quay. In picture are R. Watson outside heavy lift manager, W. Hardy steerer, W. McLean outside erecting foreman and 70 year old W. Muir formerly "Clyde's" driver.
Taken in 1948 this is the last picture of Road Engines & Kerr vehicle before nationalisation.

84. — A John Young & Co. vehicle tramcar suspended on home built trailer, 1945/6.
Tramcars were moved from Manchester to Aberdeen this way.

One of the unusual jobs that came their way at that time was to float a heavy electricity cable across Loch Awe. This was done by a tractor fitted with a winch hauling the cable placed on hundreds of barrels hired from Messrs Clark Hunter the barrel stockists in Paisley. Another unusual job which John Young & Co., specialised in but was unusual for Kerrs was to lift a piece of machinery 100 feet up on top of a building in Glasgow City Centre. Using a 120 foot jib on a Coles crane it was successfully carried out during the night.

NATIONALISATION

In late 1948 early 1949 Rail & Road transport was nationalised by Act of Parliament. Independent heavy haulage companies were exempted but as Pickfords, Road Engines and Kerr and various other English firms were owned by the Railway Companies, they themselves were nationalised. A Group of Heavy Hauliers a branch of the British Road Services was set up in England and Wales which consisted mainly of Pickfords vehicles and trailers. To save repainting all of this equipment it was agreed to call this nationalised division of B.R.S. by its old name — Pickfords.

In Glasgow the following companies came together under the new B.R.S. "Pickfords" heavy haulage banner — Road Engines & Kerr (Haulage) Ltd., Isaac Barrie & Company and the heavy haulage section of John Young & Co.

John Young & Co., 120 Kelvinhaugh Street, Glasgow originally of 282 Stobcross Street had started off with a horse and cart in 1888 as a cartage contractor. They dealt in scrap and gradually entered the erection and machinery moving business. They purchased a Foden steam wagon No. F8730 Reg. No. MA233 new in 1919 and with this machine many large but light loads were moved. This included a Y.M.C.A. hut from St. Enoch's Square to Yoker about six miles, using a bogey running on the tram rails after the last tram at night. In 1924 they moved from 282 Stobcross St., to their new address. Another Foden steam wagon arrived in 1926 No. F12104 Reg. No. ES8244. This was sold in 1933 after the arrival of a six wheeled Sentinel DG6-8738 Reg. No. HH6392 in 1932 bought from Thistle Transport of Carlisle.

ENTER "BUBBLY" YOUNG

No more steamers were purchased. As soon as Messrs Fodens started building diesels, one was taken on trial and proved to be a great success. By this time Robert nicknamed "Bubbly" the son of the founder was in charge. He had a flair for moving odd things in unorthodox ways.

In the middle thirties an American oil company who were test drilling for oil in the Lothians asked for quotations to move the rig a mile across country. Bubbly's tender was the lowest by far. The Texan engineer pointed out that it was impossible to dismantle it and re-erect it for that price, only to be told by Bubbly that he knew what he was doing. The Texan, taken aback said "Do it!"

Nearly all haulage companies including Youngs had a blacksmith on the staff but Bubbly went across the River Clyde to borrow Road Engines & Kerrs blacksmith who was used to the type of work he had in mind.

MOVING IN UNISON

William McCorquodale of Youngs and Charlie Bowie of Kerrs, with four hammermen manufactured two heavy axles and fitted them with iron wheels to carry the test rig across the fields. The job was carried out as planned. A diesel tractor fitted with a winch

85. — John Young & Company Ltd., specialised in the erection of steel chimneys. This one on a six-wheeled Foden mounted on steel trestles with erecting pole lashed to side, weighed approx 11 tons, and was 90 feet long. Glasgow to Doncaster, 1945.

hauled the rig with three ballasted four wheelers guyed to the rig moving in unison. The iron wheels were plated all the way.

The Texan took a cine record of the move saying that he had never seen anything like it before. By the outbreak of the second world war Youngs had quite a fleet of Fodens one 50 ton tractor with winch, two 50 ton articulated tractors with winch, four 30 ton articulateds, one 15 ton articulated, two flat 6 wheelers and three flat 4 wheelers, also 1 E.R.F. flat four-wheeler with 6 L.W. Gardner Engine. They had a 20 ton dockside-type level luffing crane with a 100 foot jib which could lift any of the trailers over the wall into or out of the yard.

THE FIRST OF ITS KIND

Trailers came in all sizes depending on the job to be moved. Bubbly often built trailers to suit the job with the help of his blacksmith. In 1944 he constructed a special trailer to carry the 64 ton quadruple expansion steam engines for corvettes. Built on a 50 ton six wheeled unit was a short two-axle trailer. Superimposed on the short trailer was a low loading trailer with a 23 feet well and 16 wheels at the rear on oscilliating axles. This type of trailer is fairly common today but Bubbly's was the first.

Bubbly moved the tramcars from Salford to Aberdeen on a specially constructed trailer built on to a 30 ton articulated unit. Using a turntable on top of what is known as the fifthwheel with cross H beams, a two axle monkey carried long H beams that sat on the cross H beams and the tram was suspended between them. This avoided much height to the double decked tram.

One of their specialities was moving and erecting steel chimneys. Some were very large, weighing around 30 tons. They also erected overhead cranes using heavy poles in the days before mobile cranes came into general use. Messrs Mechans of Scotstoun built steel chimneys and other large cylindrical vessels for oil refineries etc. Some of these vessels were moved by flat 4 or 6 wheelers with a monkey, the loads being over 80 foot long. Many were delivered to the south and east coasts of England.

When the European war was over two Diamond T's were purchased from war surplus sales, one a tractor, and the other articulated. Also two Loraine mobile cranes which were also U.S. Army Surplus. More Loraine cranes came and a new depot was opened at Sheffield, stocked with cranes and low loaders. With the help of the cranes, safes and fireproof filing cabinets were hoisted into offices all over the city centres in Scottish towns. Later, hinged jibs were used up to 120 feet long.

86. — A long load travelling south over a bridge on the A66 just South of Penrith 1946.

87. — A six wheeled Foden with trailing monkey taking a 120 feet long steel chimney for an oil refinery from Mechans of Glasgow to the south east of England. John Young & Co., 1946.

88. — Diamond T. and Foden tractors with two half barges being moved from the builders Milne Bros. of Paisley to Glasgow docks for shipment. J. Young & Co., 1947.

89. — A London barge moving by road up Loch Lomondside, 1947.

90. — Turning in the Colquhoun Arms car park before launching into Loch Lomond.

LOCH LOMOND

As well as the usual excavators, crushers etc, a tug boat and four barges were required to haul sand and gravel about twenty miles from Balloch at the south end of Loch Lomond to within a few miles of Ardlui at the northern end. The local council refused to allow tippers to run up the length of the loch as the road was very narrow. The tug boat "Dart" and the barges were brought up from the Thames and launched into the loch near Luss village. They were carried up on ex U.S. forces tank transporter Roger trailers.

Bubbly died and the haulage side was sold to the Nationalised Board. John Young & Co., retained their crane hire division.

91. — Tug "Dart" having funnel fitted before launching.

92. — With Diamond T. nosing the trailer into the water using his winch to steady it down assisted by the winch of a Foden tractor. The law and the people look on.

93. — Gradually "Dart" takes to the water. She hauled sand and gravel up Loch Lomond for the North of Scotland Hydro Electric Board Loch Sloy Power Scheme as the road was too narrow for tippers to operate. 1947 John Young & Co.

94. — Disaster on the Pennines when en-route from Sheffield to Liverpool with a tank locomotive for shipment.

95. — Sandy Whitelaw, outside erecting manager and a mobile crane to the rescue.
Eased up and winched over to continue the journey to Liverpool. John Young & Co., 1947.

96. — Diamond T. with home built trailer carrying a Denny built boiler along Great Western Road, Glasgow.
John Young & Co., 1947.

97. — Two Diamond T's with a big gear wheel on two trailers. John Young & Co., 1947.

98. — Two Loraine mobile cranes ex U.S. Army erecting a 42 ton turbine in Kelvinhall, Glasgow for
an engineering exhibition. John Young & Co., 1948.

Pickfords as the British Road Services Heavy Haulage Division took over where Road Engines and Kerr left off. George Mathers of Kerrs carried on as Depot Manager assisted by Alex McKinlay, for although John Young's and Isaac Barrie's vehicles, drivers and statutory attendants had joined the group, they brought no managerial staff of any kind with them. In England the various heavy haulage firms coming together to join Pickfords caused a lot of bad feeling among the driving staffs. So much so that a few drivers left for other pastures and Pickfords kept the old names up on the vehicles with the hungry lion on the doors.

In Glasgow this did not happen, as by tradition the men of the old firms had always helped one another on the road when anything went wrong even although the firms were in opposition. The coming together of the vehicles and men gave at first a surplus of both but this sorted itself out. Kerr's old hands retired, one of whom was over 70 years of age. The combined fleet had risen to one Fowler and one Burrell road locos, four Diamond T's, two 80 ton Scammells, three 50 ton Fodens, six 45 ton Scammells, three 30 ton Fodens and two Scammell tractors of approximately 35 tons, plus two 20 ton E.R.F's. As other firms were nationalised David Barrie's 45 ton Scammell from Dundee joined them plus an 80 ton Scammell and a Diamond T from Edinburgh. All these

came to Kerrs yard at Mavisbank which could not even hold Kerrs own fleet, so half lay around the docks wherever there happened to be space handy for them.

RE-ORGANISATION

Mr Irvine came up from England to be Manager for Scotland with George Mathers as Depot Manager, Alex MacKinlay Outside Manager with Bob Watson in charge of the outside squads. A selection of regular work remained, the moving of locomotives continued with the two traction engines and *Loch Ness Monster* moving from Hydepark and Queenspark Works to the docks for shipment. Tramcars from Liverpool to Glasgow, work inherited from J Young, were moved by an E.R.F. unit, suspended between H beams as J Young had done. John G Kincaids and Babcock & Wilcox work came back to Mavisbank with Isaac Barrie. Kerr's own work with Barclay Curle Ltd., Beardmore, The Steel Company of Scotland, Colvilles etc. continued to come in. Vehicles of all sizes were kept busy.

A LARGE SHIPMENT

Messrs Caledonian Steam Packet Co., the Government owned ferry operators asked Pickford to quote to move a 90 ton boat, the Countess of Breadalbane, from Loch Awe in Argyllshire to Loch Fyne and launch her ready to be towed to Greenock. Using Isaac Barrie's 32 wheeled crane trailer, the boat was winched out of the Loch onto the trailer which was standing on steel plates. Then the trailer in turn was

99. — 1st picture after nationalisation Diamond T. and Scammell 45 tons tractor with 1938 built Dyson 75 ton trailer with manual brakes. R. Watson outside erecting manager leaning on swanneck, 1949.

100. — 1929 built 100 ton Scammell ex Marsden Road Services and Edward Box now replacing the two steamers "Supreme" and "Simplicity", 1949.

winched up out of the water on to the beach, then out on to the road. The boat was 100 feet long by 17 feet 9 inches wide and 14 feet 6 inches high. It was hauled by a Scammell Pioneer traced by a 45 ton Scammell with another Pioneer standing by for winching.

THE END OF THE LINE FOR STEAM

The last of the steam traction engines were taken off the road and the ex Edward Box/MRS 100 ton Scammell built in **1929** replaced them, with a crew of three instead of six. The 100 ton vehicle had been built to carry railway locomotives from the Vulcan works at Newton le Willows, Lancashire to Liverpool docks. Rails were built into the trailer well in several gauges which suited the North British Locomotive Co. This vehicles worked until the North British closed down in the mid sixties.

About this time Pickfords moved from Mavisbank to the old meat haulage yard in Fleming Street off Duke Street in the east end. George Mathers retired and Alex MacKinlay was made up to Depot Manager. The old Diamond T's were replaced by Scammell Constructors as were the Pioneers and at a later date Super Constructors arrived for the heavy loads. Although new Crane trailers were also acquired the old Isaac Barrie 32 wheeler continued to be used because of its low height.

THE CHANGING SCENE

The firm had now reached its peak as far as employing men, as forty were on the books. (In Kerr's day it averaged thirty). This too at the time when new firms were setting up in business in heavy haulage which was still not nationalised. These included Sandy Gilmour, shifting earth-moving machinery mostly but taking the odd industrial movement. The Glasgow Hiring Co. Ltd., taking up to 30 tons mostly for Sir William Arrol Ltd., crane division in Rigby Street, Parkhead, with a few excavators for the Glasgow Corporation.

McKelvie/Strathclyde Transport started with an eight-cylinder Gardner engined Foden and a 120 ton trailer. They undercut Pickfords rate to Cochrane of Annan for a large vessel to Grangemouth. This movement was carried out during the Glasgow Fair Holidays.

As part of the route was over the A74 which was being reconstructed at the time, a considerable hold up was caused, at one time the tailback stretched fourteen miles. It was after this that the company name was changed to Strathclyde Transport Services and they operated from Motherwell. Most of their work was with the Steel Company of Scotland at Hallside and Craigneuk moving ingots and heavy steel plate. Also they took numerous loads from the Motherwell Bridge and Engineering Co. Ltd.

101. — Another view of the 100 ton Scammell with streering and braking cabin at rear in 1949 with a 2-8-2 locomotive on board. for the Spanish National Railways. Driven by George Burns back steered by Tom McIntosh ex-McLaren driver and Ronald Bell statutory attendant. J.G. Kincaids Albion artic is in the foreground.

102. — Pioneer Scammell with 32 wheeled crane trailer carrying a 2-6-6-2 electric locomotive for the South African Railways and Harbour Board at Queens Park Works 1949.

103. — 0-8-0 for Emu Bay Railway (Tasmania) loaded on a 50 tons trailer 1950.

Gavin Wilkie of Boden Street, Glasgow was another who entered the field. This company had been Cartage contractors from the last century, only entering into heavy haulage in the late 1940's. They worked mainly for Sir Wm. Arrol the crane and bridge builders and various construction companies. They operated two fifty ton Scammell constructors with a 100 ton trailer plus four Scammell articulateds around the 30 ton mark. They sold out to Pickford in 1974.

When the indivisible loading law was increased to 32 tons this brought more firms into the operation. Kaye Goodfellow of Manchester opened a depot and clearing house in the east end of Glasgow. Cawthorn Sinclair from the Tyneside moved into Uddingston with a clearing house. The Caterpillar Tractor Co. at Tannochside built tractors some of which were under 21 tons which could be loaded on general haulage 40 feet trailers for shipment. These two clearing houses moved into Caterpiller taking most of the work from Pickford. General Motors opened a factory at Newhouse to build giant earth-moving trucks, these were run to the docks by Scotia Services of Elliot Street, Glasgow who had opened in 1946 to erect and dismantle machinery. Later this work was taken on by the West of Scotland Transport of Newarthill who operate Mack units.

The coming of the Volvo's, MAN's, DAF's, Scania's and U.S.A built units knocked Scammell out until they increased their tractors capacities. With new Continental trailers by King-Schuerle and modular trailers built by Nicolas where sections could be added or subtracted as was required with hydraulic jacks built into each section along with air brakes. Swan necks now came fitted with hydraulic rams driven by a Petters diesel engine mounted on the flat above the swan neck, to lift the well section of the trailer. When withdrawing two pins the front of the well can be lowered to the ground disconnected and the unit moves forward with the swan neck leaving the well clear to load a tracked or wheeled machine. This takes about five minutes. This tremendous time saving with the new units and trailers meant that the heavy hauliers had to re-equip or go out.

Now from Glasgow to Southampton with approximately 70 tons of reasonable dimensions, the vehicle leaves one day and delivers the next day using motorways practically all the way. Prior to this, the time taken was anything up to three weeks, via the A1 road.

Continued on page 98.

104. — Two views of the former Isaac Barrie, Pioneer 80 ton Scammells and 32 wheeled crane trailer with prefabricated bedplate and crankshaft 1949/50. 110 tons. J. G. Kincaid of Greenock.

105. — The same outfit again with a Diamond T. shoving at the back at the "Rest and be Thankful" in Argyllshire with an 80 ton stator en-route to Glen Shira Power Station 1950.

106. — Pickford's Diamond T. with 80 ton dredger from Paisley to Hull 1955.

107. — Pioneer traced by 45 ton Scammell tractor with "Countess of Breadalbane" 110 feet x 17 feet 9 inches x 14 feet 6 inches high. Moving from Loch Awe to be launched into Loch Fyne in April 1952.

108. — Scammell carrying funnel over old bridge at Haydon Bridge,
Northumberland with an inch and a half clearance on either side, 1954.

109. — Passing through Liverpool, 1954 with steam accumulator from Annan.

110. — Loading at the Motherwell Bridge and Engineering Company.

111. — 102 tons, 97 feet 8 inches long, 13 feet wide, the Pioneer moves out for Grangemouth, 1955.

112. — Internal works in John Browns yard, 146 tons, 1960.

113. — Sternframe from Colvilles, Clydebridge to Havertonhill, Co. Durham. All sternframes were
loaded, canted like this to cut down the width and had to be tied on before the crane let go. 45 tons
loaded on a Dyson ex-British Army tank trailer, 1960.

114. — View from nearside, 39 feet 6 inches long x
19 feet 10 inches wide and 6 feet high.

115. — 45 ton Scammell tractor with 30 tons of cased aircompressor for export
from Alley and McLellan of Polmadie, 1958.

116. — 100 ton casting from Beardmore, Glasgow for delivery to Robertson of Bedford.
Two Super Constructors with 150 tons trailer, 1960.

117. — 1971, two Super Contractors with two 32 wheeled solid-tyred trailers carry 225 tons.

118. — The same outfit again loading on to a Ro-Ro boat.

119. — The heavy left ship with its **300** ton derrick picks up
another similar load for the near East.

120. — A load from Motherwell Bridge Engineering, 53 feet long, 29 feet 6 inches in diameter tapering to 13 feet 6 inches, 59 tons from Linthouse to King George V Dock for Come by Chance Refinery, New Foundland. August 1972.

121. — 300 ton Reactor being winched on to Heavy Lift Vessel at Princess Dock.

122. — Unloading at Grangemouth.

123. — Running to the refinery with R. Whitlock outside heavy lift supervisor walking
and A. MacKinlay riding on tractor.

124. — Three Super Contractors hauling 355 tons including the trailer from Rosyth to Kincardine for Longannet Power Station.

HEAVIEST EVER
THIS 270-TON
GENERATOR TRANSFORMER
AND ITS 85-ton TRANSPORTER
ARE GOING FROM
BRUCE PEEBLES LTD., EDINBURGH,
TO LONGANNET POWER STATION, FIFE—
OVER THE FORTH FROM
GRANTON TO ROSYTH
IN THE
KINGSNORTH FISHER
A SPECIALLY BUILT "ROLL ON, ROLL OFF"
SHIP.
355 TONS TAKE SOME MOVING
SORRY IF YOU'VE BEEN HELD UP.

125. — The sign tells it all.

126. — 200 feet high, 200 tons in weight moved from East Yard Port Glasgow to the Kingston Basin approx 1 mile. One week's work with all other traffic off the road when load was moving and all overhead wires down but it saved three months dismantling and re-erection.
127. — Passing a partly complete tanker.

128. — With a new 1965 trailer bound for Finland on a Ro-Ro Ship.

129. — 180 tons on another new King trailer.

130. — Lonmay Village Aberdeenshire did not know what had happened to it, when Pickford passed through en-route from Fraserburgh to St. Fergus in 1978.

131. — The overhead bridge carrying the main railway line had to be raised from 14 feet 3 inches to 22 feet 6 inches to allow this column to proceed.

132. — 205 tons, 138 feet 9 inches x 15 feet 10 inches wide x 15 feet 9 inches high plus height of Nicolas trailer took many slow hours through the village.

133. — 500 ton boat floated on to trailer then hauled into shed to allow workers to reconstruct without loss of time during sub zero weather.

134. — Out of the water.

135. — Into the shed at Scott Lithgow, Greenock.

136. — From Babcock Power Ltd., for the U.S.S.R. 215 tons 17.6m long, 5.5m wide and 6.2m high. One of four shipped 1979.

137. — 1082 tons 90 feet long, 55 feet wide and 60 feet high. Motherwell Bridge (Offshore)Ltd., from Western Harbour Leith to barge for Chevron Oil using 4 — 240 ton Scammell Contractors. July 1977.

138. — Many wheels make light work -- especially below a thousand and eighty-two tons.

139. — Strathclyde Transport of Motherwell with a Foden tractor hauling a
68 ton vessel from Annan to Grangemouth in the mid 1960's.

140. — A telegraph pole poses an awkward problem as Strathclyde Transport make their way from
Annan to Seal Sands on the Tees-side with a column 100 feet long in the mid 1960's.

141. — Motherwell Bridge Engineering Ltd., Project Division with a collection of pipes and valves
for the oil industry. Hauled by Strathclyde Transport, 1970.

142. — A large load from Motherwell Bridge to Newfoundland, weighing 38 tons,
hauled by Strathclyde, 1972.

143. — An even larger load from Motherwell Bridge going to Glasgow docks for export, 1970's.

144. — Strathclyde Transport could move up to 225 tons. Here is one of the capacity
loads moved with Volvo tractor units.

Early in 1982 Pickfords was denationalised and bought out by the employees, forming a consortium with no outside financial help. Once again the Pickfords name was retained, saved repainting all the plant. It is now Pickfords Industrial Ltd., part of the National Freight Consortium PLC.

The current recession has hit the heavy haulage with firms disappearing which had been household names. Beardmore of Parkhead closed down their last bastion on the Clydeside — a firm that once employed 40,000 men, gone.

The Steel Company of Scotland at Craigneuk and Hallside under British Steel closed, and with them went Strathclyde Transport who closed and the vehicles went back to McKelvie of Paisley where they are doing some heavy haulage with new trailers. Clyde Bridge Iron and Steel Works formerly Colvilles shut because of lack of plate orders from shipbuilding firms. Shipbuilding firms are practically non existent, a mere shadow of the old Clydeside. Gone are David Rowan, Barclay Curle, Harland & Wolf, A & J Inglis, Stephens, John Brown, Denny, Lobnitz, Simons, Fleming & Ferguson, the Blythswood, C. Connal also A. F. Craig, Wilson of Lillybank, Penmans, Glengarnock and all the ancillary firms and sub-contractors. Left are Upper Clyde Shipbuilders including Yarrow, Browns old yard with an oil rig builder, Ailsa Ferguson, Scott Lithgow. J. G. Kincaid, Babcocks & Wilcox, Motherwell Bridge & Engineering, J. Brown Engineering and the only locomotive builder left in Scotland, Barclay in Kilmarnock.

Over the past fifteen years heavy haulage contractors have come and gone. Gavin Wilkie sold out to Pickford, Sandy Gilmour just gave up. The Glasgow Hiring gave up too, with newcomers W.H. Malcolm of Brookfield and Cadzow Plant of Hamilton.

Pickfords staff have been cut to twenty four with eight units plus the big trailers. They have Bruce Peebles the transformer builders of Edinburgh along with oil rig yards on the east coast, where some big lifts have taken place 1,100 tonnes, an oil module, from Leith Harbour loaded on to a barge using four 240 ton gross train weight tractors, the new Contractors by Scammell built to beat the foreign competition.

The new Pickfords team in Glasgow are J. S. Banks, General Manager and J Parkinson, Depot Manager which replaced Alex MacKinlay, Heavy Lift Manager and Bob Whitlock, Outside Manager, who had been given early retirement before the denationalisation.

However a number of progressive firms who have re-equipped and increased their efficiency have weathered the recession and offer a service better than

145. — Cadzow Plant moving the "Countess Fiona" from Stobcross Crane to Loch Lomond. Strange to relate the same hull was moved in April 1952, thirty years previously, then the "Countess of Breadalblane." (See photo 107).

ever. Cadzow Plant Hire Ltd., of Hamilton changed from tipping truck operators to heavy haulage contractors in 1977. Started with new Scanias then moved on to Volvos F10 and F12 with fluid flywheel. Purchased new hydraulic swan necked demount trailers, the heaviest being a 120 tons capacity Tasker. The trailer is articulated with two additional axles at the front which turn with the unit. Having a loading length of 24 feet at 2 feet 5 inches high and 49 feet 5 inches at 3 feet 6 inches high with five axles at the rear which steer automatically and also fitted with a hydraulic swan neck. The height at the rear can be lowered to suit bridge heights.

Strange to relate at the end of the forties Pickford moved the "Countess of Breadalbane" from Loch Awe to Inverary. Now with her name changed to the "Countess Fiona" this trailer and a F12 Volvo moved her from Stobcross Crane in Glasgow to Balloch, Loch Lomond in 1982. Weighing 80 tons only on the last move. With the short trailer she had an overhang of 45 feet at the rear. On arrival at Balloch she was run head first down to the water edge then the unit and swan neck removed when with 12 inch square keel blocks from 20 feet long downwards built under the boat to allow the trailer to be pulled out from the rear then she was launched into the Loch.

Also strange to relate giant presses and anvil blocks put into Ayr Stampworks in 1942 by Road Engines & Kerr (Haulage) Ltd., have been dismantled and Cadzow have moved several loads down to Merseyside.

146. — Hydraulic swan-neck removed to allow machine to walk on to the 120 ton trailer at Cadzow Plant.

147. — Swan-neck replaced, pumped up ready for the road. Cadzow Plant, 1983.

Thanks to the following who kindly allowed us to reproduce their photographs:

Babcock International p.l.c. 55, 119, 121, 122, 123, 128, 129, 136. Balfour Beatty & Co. Ltd. 34, 35, 36, 37, 39, 40, 41, 42, 43, 44, 48, 49, 50, 51, 52, 53, 54. Andrew Barclay Sons & Co. Ltd. 1, 18. R.A.D. Bennison M.I.Mech.E. Front Cover (top). Dr. D.K.M. Black M.D.Ch.B 15, 46, 47, 58, 59, 60, 61, 62, 63, 64, 65, 69, 75, 76, 83. Cadzow Plant Hire Ltd. Front Cover (bottom) 145, 146, 147. Clyde Port Authority 73, 77. Cochranes of Annan 29. W. Lind Esq. 12, 13, 22, 56, 57, 66. Mrs E. McDougall 7. D. McKay Esq. 9, 16. McKelvie & Co. (Transport) Ltd. 140, 141. Mitchell Library, Glasgow 24, 25, 27, 31, 32, 33, 33A, 70 71, 79, 80, 101, 102, 103. Motherwell Bridge Fabricators Ltd. 137, 138, 139, 142, 143, 144. Museum of Transport, Glasgow 3, 8. N.E.I. Peebles Ltd. 124, 125. T.B. Paisley Collection 2, 10, 11, 14, 19, 20, 21, 23, 26, 28, 29A, 30, 38, 78, 81, 82. Pickfords Industrial Ltd. 4, 5, 67, 99, 100, 104, 105, 106, 107, 108, 109, 112, 113, 114, 117, 118, 120, 126, 127, 130, 131, 132, 133, 134, 135. W. Ralston Ltd. 17, 74, 98, 110, 111, 115, 116. Road Locomotive Society 6, 45, 68. Weir Pumps Ltd. 72. John Young & Co. (Kelvinhaugh) Ltd. 84, 85, 86, 87, 88, 89, 90, 91, 92, 93, 94, 95, 96, 97.　　　　T. McT.

First Published in 1985
by Alloway Publishing Ltd.,
24 Beresford Terrace, Ayr.
Reprinted 1988

Printed in Scotland
by Walker & Connell Ltd.,
Hastings Square, Darvel,
Ayrshire.

ISBN 0 907526 17 9

CONDITIONS OF SALE

PIONEERS OF HEAVY HAULAGE

T. McTaggart

Alloway Publishing
AYR

TO ALL THE HEAVY HAULAGE MEN
WHO HAVE GONE AHEAD.

PIONEERS OF HEAVY HAULAGE

T. McTaggart